Let It Grow!

We are rediscovering that the only way to reach all the people in a culturally diverse culture is through multi-congregational churches. Josh Hunt has stated this concept in terms of biblical context and in pragmatic detail. Don't miss this bright, readable, powerful book.

Charles Chaney
Vice President, Home Mission Board of the Southern Baptist Convention
Co-author, *Design for Church Growth*

I agree with Josh 100 percent that multiple use of buildings and resources is good stewardship and it is the very best way to fulfill the Great Commission.

Dale Galloway
Senior Pastor, New Hope Community Church
Portland, Oregon

Josh Hunt's book should be read by all who are looking for new ways to reach people in the 1990s.

Rick Warren
Saddleback Valley Community Church
Mission Viejo, California

The idea of the multi-congregation church portends the future . . . especially in the great metropolitan areas. We need to start literally thousands in areas where the cost of land and construction is prohibitive.

Larry Lewis
President, Home Mission Board of the Southern Baptist Convention

Josh has written a challenging work worth every church leader's consideration. The church of today will be impotent by the year 2000 unless some present paradigms are challenged. Josh is pioneering this challenge.

Randy Pope
Pastor, Perimeter Church, Atlanta, Georgia

Josh Hunt shows the whys and hows of the multi-congregation church—an emphasis vastly needed on today's church growth terrain. Here at last we find the imperative emphasis and detailed guidance for overcoming the "edifices complex." This book could turn around the dilemma of falling growth rates in many denominations. *Let It Grow!* may well be the . . . most significant contribution to the church growth field in the last decade—perhaps ever.

Ebbie Smith
Professor of Ethics and Missions
Southwestern Baptist Theological Seminary, Fort Worth, Texas
Author, *Balanced Church Growth*

Let It Grow!

Changing to Multi-Congregation Churches

Josh Hunt

Foreword by John N. Vaughan

BAKER
BOOK HOUSE

Box 6287, Grand Rapids, Michigan 49516-6287

Published by Baker Book House Company
P. O. Box 6287, Grand Rapids, Michigan 49516-6287

Printed in the United States of America

Library of Congress Cataloging-in-Publication Data

Hunt, Josh.
    Let it grow! : changing to multi-congregation churches / Josh Hunt.
       p.   cm.
    Includes bibliographical references.
    ISBN 0–8010–4377–8
    1. Church growth. 2. Church meetings. I. Title.
    BV652.25.H835   1993
    254—dc20   92-29511

To

Bill Sloan

who challenged me

to read my first book

and to write my first book

Contents

Foreword

Two years ago I had never heard the name Josh Hunt; neither had we met. However, after our first telephone conversation together, we became friends with intense mutual interests in several topics. One of those topics was the central theme of this book: multi-congregational churches.

Various forms of this type of congregational structure are mentioned in my book, *The World's 20 Largest Churches* (Baker, 1984). Such congregations tend to have an average weekly worship attendance of over 10,000 persons. Most of these churches are beyond the borders of the United States. Almost all have some type of highly developed network of satellite ministries and/or congregations with a separate staff organization related structurally to the mother congregation.

Josh Hunt and Sam Shaw, the senior pastor at Calvary Baptist Church of Las Cruces, New Mexico, represent an increasing number of church leaders who now conduct three or more worship services each weekend. This book identifies both practical and theoretical issues faced by any congregation or staff leadership team committed to reaching a number of unconverted and other unchurched people far exceeding the seating capacity of their present worship center. At the heart of this issue is also the mandate to effectively nurture, teach, equip, mobilize, and multiply the saints already actively involved within these congregations.

The "multi-congregation" concept is the next step beyond traditional multiple-staff and multiple-services. Pastors, other staff members, and congregations are crossing new frontiers with very few models that understand essential growth decisions. This book will help them. Churches who lack either interest in continued growth or a sense of Great Commission mandate will benefit from reading these pages. This book is definitely not Church Growth 101 for the novice church-leader but the help it gives is written in a clear, well-focused, and understandable manner.

Whether your interest is in the biblical definition of a New Testament church, reaching target groups through effective marketing strategies, mobilizing church members, avoiding staff burn-out, developing master-planning, or breaking previously intimidating growth barriers, this book will help expand your vision and understanding to that of a church staff team that has already led its congregation to having five worship services each weekend. The concepts taught in these pages, though simple and biblical, exceed both the vision and training of staff teams even in many large churches. I commend this book to you. It could prove to be the most vital church growth book you will read in the twentieth century!

John N. Vaughan
Editor of *Church Growth Today*

Acknowledgments

I'd like to thank the many people who helped me make this project a reality. First and foremost, my wife, Sharon, not only put up with my hibernation and addiction to this material but also carefully proofread every sentence. She spoke the truth in love and made this a better book.

I am grateful to the church, Calvary Baptist Church of Las Cruces, New Mexico, where I am allowed to pursue the vision.

Many other people read the manuscript and made suggestions at various stages: Shelby Bacuum, Lance Witt, James Clark, Susan Wright, Darla Hapgood, Jeff Wagner, Bill Sloan, Sam Shaw, Andy Randall, Lamar Moren, Gene O. Jamison, David Edwards, Don Cartlidge, Marti and Carl Nelson, and Walter and Aliene Hunt. I appreciate the help they have given.

Thanks to the staff at Baker Book House, including Betty De Vries, Dan Knight, and Paul Engle, for their suggestions and work on this book.

Introduction

A Thesis and a Dream

A legitimate model for the New Testament church was to have daily gatherings and believers in both small groups and large. An individual Christian would not attend *all* of these meetings, but was probably present each week at one or two large-group meetings and one or two small-group meetings. Because multiple pastors led the large groups, no one person preached seven days a week. Although each pastor may have preached more than once during that time span, this arrangement minimized the fatigue factor for a pastor and other church "staff" (elders and deacons, for example). The early church could be described as a multi-congregation church—a cluster of congregations, each one separate, yet part of the whole.

Following this model would have significant impact on our ability to respond to the calling that God placed upon us: the Great Commission. I believe that this one change in church life may be as important as any single Christian movement since William Carey. If the multi-congregation church, perhaps meeting daily, is allowed by Scripture and would make us more effective in "making disciples of all nations" (see Matt. 28:19–20), a reasonable course of action is to explore this possibility fully. In fact, it is my thesis that we should pursue with all diligence whatever ideas and plans would move us toward becoming a nation of multi-congregation churches.

During a certain quiet time, I began meditating on several passages from the Book of Acts that speak explicitly of the church as meeting every day (this will be discussed further in chapter 3). The idea came to me that this probably did not mean that *everyone* met every day, but that church meetings were being conducted on a daily basis. The average church member probably attended about as often as he or she does now each week: one or two large-group meetings and one or two small-group meetings. It occurred to me that adopting this model of the early church would have profound impact on the way we "do church," and would greatly increase our effectiveness in terms of the Great Commission.

Through the coming months, as I continued to meditate on this idea, we discussed it on numerous occasions in staff meetings. One of the things that came up in these discussions is that this idea was not as original with me as I had thought. Sam Shaw, my pastor, had actually been persuading me in that direction after he attended a conference at the Fuller Church Growth Institute, led by Carl George. George had pointed out that many churches today (and he foresees the trend more and more in the future) have many services with several preaching pastors. The question Sam asked me was, "Why couldn't we have ten or fifteen services a week?" After several months, Sam asked me to write a paper describing the multi-congregation church.

This book, originally written as a paper for internal use in our church, is the result of Sam's request. I have a strong conviction that this idea may be truly inspired by God. It is solidly biblical and rooted in prayer. It has as its objective the fulfilling of the Great Commission. This is not a perfect plan, nor is it a panacea. It would not so much cause a particular church to grow as it would remove the barriers to growth and encourage discipleship. I ask you to give careful consideration to this model for the modern church. It may be a breakthrough idea whose time has come. Perhaps God has put us here for just such a purpose: to redefine the way the church thinks about "doing church."

I have a dream that we give to the next generation a much more effective means of fulfilling the Great Commission, a responsibility placed on every Christian.

Part One

Exploring the Multi-Congregation Model

1

A Tale of an American Church

Meet Harry, an average stereotypical American. He is the "Unchurched Harry"[1] we Christians are trying to go after. Harry is relatively content, even smug about his current state of life. He has a good job with a stable income and is married to Mary, who is his second wife. Mary brought two children by a previous marriage to the relationship, and she and Harry have parented one child. Harry has a couple of kids of his own who live with their mother, and he pays what he thinks is an "unreasonable" amount of child support. His key values are financial success, family, and recreation—in short, "the good life," the American Dream.

How can we reach Harry with the gospel? Furthermore, how will we develop a system that will self-perpetuate itself and reach more and more unchurched people like him? It is not as difficult as you might think. The key to reaching Harry is to discover a felt need and show him how the gospel relates to it. In other words, show him how the gospel will make him more successful at reaching his goals. (People come to Christ for *their* reasons, not ours.) Topics like "How to Have a Better Marriage," "Managing Your Money," "How to Set Goals and Reach Them," and "Becoming a Better Friend" find a ready audience with Harry.

There is a whole new generation of churches that have demonstrated that Harry is not a lost cause. These churches couch the gospel in contemporary language. They use up-to-date illustrations, surround him with people who look like him, use music that he can relate to, get his attention through media advertising, make the message speak practically to his everyday situation, and provide quality child care and youth programs for his children. Also, they do *not* talk too much about money! If we give Harry some time, and most of all, give him anonymity, we can reach him. And he will be our most effective evangelist. He has lots of unchurched friends and, as a satisfied customer, he will be more than willing to tell them about his discovery.

Look down the road a bit—beyond Harry's conversion and initial discipleship—and try to answer these questions:

- If Harry is reachable, why are 80 percent of the churches in America not reaching him?
- If one in four unchurched Americans would be in church this weekend if a friend would invite them,[2] why are we so ineffective in getting them there?
- Why are there no more people claiming to be born-again Christians today than there were several years ago?[3]
- What happened to churches that were once growing with people like Harry, but now seldom see a bona fide outsider enter their fold?
- In short, what is wrong with the system?

Project it out. Suppose Harry is reached by a 25-year-old church in Suburbia, USA, that is using direct mail, a variety of music formats (Harry loves variety), and contemporary, relative preaching. What happens when this church, "Trinity Church" we will call it, begins bulging with Harrys? Very predictably, two things will occur. First, the members will engage in the classic pioneer/homesteader battle.[4] Second, they will initiate a building campaign and fund-raising drive. These two events are so predictable, you can schedule them on the calendar. Write them down; they will happen, as surely as a spring revival or Vacation Bible School.

The Pioneer/Homesteader Battle

The pioneers founded the church by giving large sums of money and a great sacrifice of time to ensure its survival. They have high values for the denomination and for tradition. They have a network of friends within the church who have enjoyed one another's company for decades. Their children were married here. They have buried some from among them. These long-time members have vivid memories of great revivals and works of God in this place. They created the liturgy that the church uses and by now have memorized it. They typify the good people whom God has used greatly to establish a whole generation of churches across our land. They like Trinity Church just the way it is and are suspicious of changes.

Enter a new pastor. He is thirty-four years old and sensitive to this group's needs—he has come to be *their* pastor, *their* spiritual leader. He also has a sense of calling to reach the not-yet-reached Harrys in the surrounding community. He adds a new service with the kind of approach that will appeal to Harry. And Harry comes. Because Harry brings his friends, after a couple of years this church is filled with Harrys, along with their wives, and children. The nursery is getting crowded, as is the parking lot. Expenses are up. Harry—a homesteader—has different values than do the pioneers. He does not remember the early struggles to survive. Conflict is on the way. This church (and its pastor) is on a collision course with disaster as battle lines are drawn between traditionalist and innovator.

There are no easy answers when pioneers and home-steaders are at odds, but there are a couple of possibilities. In essence, *together* they must redream the original dream of the church. The pastor needs to demonstrate how the current growth is a fulfillment of the goals this church has always held. He needs to pay the price of acknowledging those who have built this church. Yes, they do have only one vote each, but he had better recognize that they have more influence than that, and they deserve more respect than that. However, just as surely as the pioneers must be heard loud and clear, the church needs to develop a structure that allows new people to be involved in every area of its ministry. New members should rotate on the church board and serve as deacons and on key committees. More than anything else, these groups need to talk to each other. It is not enough for the pastor to express the views of the homesteaders to the pioneers, and vice versa. They need to talk face-to-face, to find a way to celebrate their diversity and their common Lord.

The Money Trap

Let me make the big assumption that, by the grace of God, Trinity Church makes it through this white-water period. There are bigger rapids downstream. The B (Building) word will soon cause its members to talk entirely too much about the M (Money) word, for eventually this church will run out of space. It may go to two or three services, but if it keeps meeting needs, it will need more physical facilities. The stamina of the pastor becomes the next limiting factor. He can only preach a limited number of times, and experience shows this to be about four or five times a week.

If he goes beyond this, he will not have the strength to give the church the kind of visionary leadership that has fueled its growth.

So, Trinity Church takes the only logical option available. Its leaders make plans to build. They consult with various denominational and independent consultants and are led to believe that they will be able to plan for a project totaling two or three times their annual budget. Confidently, they dive in.

What they do not know is that there are some dangerous land mines down this road. It is a truism that a building program will normally kill the pastor and stymie the growth of the church. That is, the pastor is very likely to resign (often with a large debt left behind) or leave the ministry altogether, and the church will cease to be an aggressively growing entity. It will join the ranks of the has-beens, the also-rans—the 80 percent of churches in America that are plateaued or declining.

Why is a major building campaign so often disastrous? What are these land mines? *First, the church will talk about money far more than Harry is comfortable with.* For one thing, Harry is generally suspicious of institutions, having lived through Vietnam and Watergate. His classmates' names grace the walls of the Vietnam memorial. They are not faceless names to him—they are his friends. For what? For their country, or for a government that was proved to be dishonest? Sure, he remembers the wrong being righted and the liar being caught. Justice reigned, but Harry's friends are still dead and he remains cynical about institutional goals and promises.

Harry has also lived through the scandals of televangelism. He heard touching stories from TV preachers about their need for money. He felt his own heart tugged by stories about children in need and missionaries who desperately needed financing. Then, he saw some of these same ministers being taken away to jail, having stolen millions from sincere but misguided contributors.

Further, Harry has financial pressures of his own. He has a family to support and a lifestyle he wishes to maintain. All the modern trinkets he has collected—CD player, camcorder, big screen TV, fax, home computer, VCR, microwave, Walkman, exercise equipment, cellular phone, Nintendo for the kids, a spacious house, and shiny late-model cars—have him financed near his limit. Even if bought on credit, the minimum balance owed on these items takes a good chunk of his monthly income, sizable though it is.

Yes, the leaders at Trinity Church will have to lay it on pretty hard, as any who have gone through a building program can attest. They have their own personal pressures, but must also do mailings, sermons, home visits, banquets, inserts, testimonies, Sunday-school lessons. The message is the same in them all: We want your money. Not that they do not have good reason, for this is the kingdom we are talking about here. (Or is it?)

There is a second major reason this project can detonate an explosion so nasty it can throw the train into the ravine: *People cannot decide what they want to build.* If raising money causes conflict, spending it can cause more. Some people want a gym; others want fixed pews. Some want racquetball; others want a music hall. Some want athletics; others want aesthetics. Some want a bride's room; others want a kitchen. Some want their church mean and lean; others want it tall and shiny. We don't all see our church from the same perspective, because we individualize the needs we believe it should meet.

I am not saying that compromises are impossible, that these decisions cannot be made and that the money cannot be raised. It can be done. Many churches stand as monuments to fund-raising possibilities. But, in all too many cases, they stand as empty monuments. A few congregations successfully complete a building program and keep right on growing. It happens often enough to convince us that *our* church might be able to pull it off, too. Even a slot machine sometimes pays off, so we are tempted to gamble with the odds. But the exceptions prove the rule. Normally, when a church builds a building, that will stop the growth of the church and wound or kill the pastor.

Why? Because to get new facilities built, the church must quit doing what it was doing before. The conversation in budget meetings will go something like this: "I know, it would be nice if we could do that singles retreat, that youth project, and that parenting seminar, but we have a building to pay for. And we can't spend money on advertising and evangelism this year either." Or this one: "We are all being asked to tighten our belts; maybe the church should tighten its belt, too." That sounds reasonable, until you think about it a second time. Then it occurs to you that the exact opposite dynamic is present in a church as is present in our personal budgets. At home, it is a virtue to refrain from spending, especially if we refrain from spending at home *so that* we can spend at church—so that we can do ministry. The policy at church is not one of restraint. It is doing everything we can possibly afford to do to help people. We try to do it prudently, but we do as much as possible nonetheless.

Return to Harry. He used to be excited about inviting friends to church. Now he is afraid they will be asked for money. Though the bankers beckon, Harry will still be there, still serving and still giving. But he isn't excited like he used to be and he may not even be aware of this. He once invited people constantly, but not now. There simply is not that emotional enthusiasm anymore. He is secretly afraid they will come, and he will be embarrassed because of a pressured appeal for money.

Visit the pastor. He is discouraged. He used to be excited about laying out a year-long church-growth plan. But no more. He is laying out this year's third stewardship drive and reminding himself that stewardship is part of the Christian life. He is also polishing up his résumé.

Meet Mr. Pioneer. The pastor has called on him to serve on two key committees: fund raising and construction management. He is tired. Though he used to enjoy visiting newcomers in the community, now it is just a chore. He remembers the good old exciting days when the church was growing. The budget was going up, but the bills were being paid, attendance was up, and people were joining. He wonders what happened.

Meet Mrs. Homesteader. She doesn't quite understand it. She can't put her finger on it, but this church does not quite have the friendly atmosphere it used to have. People seem a bit edgy. The pastor has been dropping hints in every message about money. We used to add staff fairly regularly, but now there seem to be some serious programming needs that are going unmet. She wonders what went wrong with the church she joined so enthusiastically five years ago. Color her out of here.

Listen to the visiting evangelist. He pinpoints the problem as sin, apathy, lukewarmness. He smells the Laodicean syndrome all over the place and lets everyone know. "If you just loved Jesus and cared for the lost, all this would not have happened! Repent and return!"

Talk to a church consultant. He says, "These people need to witness more. Perhaps a seminar on witnessing would be helpful."

Meet the denominational executive. He has observed that new churches grow for a while and then plateau, but he reasons, "Let's start more churches."

Walk with me a little farther. Where will Trinity Church be five, ten, and twenty years down the road? Growth will lessen and membership will plateau and then begin to decline. They will have a very attractive but empty building. This is the story of thousands of churches across America. Now let me ask you, "Whose fault is it?" I want to suggest that the system itself is flawed. It is no one's fault.

There has to be a better way to "do church" than this. And there is. A way that reaches a new generation of believers and allows the church to grow naturally, without the strain of excessive building programs and fund-raising drives. It is not often true in life, but it is in this case: the paradigm is both better and less expensive. Let it grow, let it grow, let it grow! To discover this way, we must go back to the beginning. The very beginning.

2

Three Kinds of Churches

It is abundantly clear that the early church employed the multi-congregation model. This does not prove anything or mean we have to change, but it is informative and may be significant. No less a scholar than John R. W. Stott has recognized this: "We notice [the form of pastoral oversight] was both local and plural—local in that the elders were chosen from within the congregation, not imposed from without, and plural in that *the familiar modern pattern of 'one pastor one church' was simply unknown*"[1] [emphasis added]. And again, "There is no biblical warrant for either the one man band (a single pastor playing all the instruments of the orchestra himself) or for a hierarchical or pyramidal structure in the local church (a single pastor perched at the apex of the pyramid)."[2] It is the subject of the next chapter to look at this matter in detail, but before we do, let's define our terms.

In this chapter I will explain what is meant by the traditional model, the multi-service model, and the multi-congregation model. These are three different *paradigms* of church life. I like Joel Barker's definition of paradigm as "a set of rules and regulations (written or unwritten) that does two things: (1) it establishes or defines boundaries; and (2) it tells you how to behave inside the boundaries in order to be successful."[3] Every church has certain rules that "good people" follow. If you don't follow the rules, you are excluded from the group. In the early seventies, hippies were coming to Christ by the thousands. But the rules of most churches said that you could not be a follower of Christ unless you had short hair, dressed conservatively, and liked organ music. This paradigm excluded hippies from all but a few of our churches. On the other hand, Chuck Smith's church (Calvary Chapel, Costa Mesa) had a different paradigm, a less restrictive set of rules. Here you could have long hair, wear sandals (or no shoes at all), worship God with guitar music and, in general, act as if appearance and lifestyle did not necessarily reveal the depth of one's faith.

Just as paradigms change in the marketplace and other aspects of our culture, so also are "rules" subject to revision in the church. In fact, the vitality, if not the survival, of any institution demands flexibility.

In the early part of this century, the Santa Fe Railroad was a giant in the transportation business, and no one questioned its dominance. Then a new technology made it possible to fly from Dallas to New York in three hours instead of spending three days on a train, and the customer was willing to pay a premium to do that. The paradigm shifted—and the Santa Fe was left behind because it could no longer satisfy the transportation "rules."

"Swiss-made" once spoke of the finest quality watches in the world. The Swiss dominated the international watch market for years. They had invented the minute hand and the second hand and were on the cutting edge of waterproofing. In 1968, they controlled more than 65 percent of the unit sales and 80 percent of the profits. Then the paradigm shifted. Precision gears, springs, and fine-tuned mechanical parts didn't help when the world went electronic. In 1968, Japan had about 1 percent of the world's watch market; today they control 33 percent. With its electronic quartz watches, Japan was able to capitalize on a change from the traditional idea of how watches should be made.

One paradigm of the church sees it as operating services on Sunday mornings; another model sees the church as confronting people whenever and wherever it can. One paradigm has rules that exclude the use of drums or guitars in worship; another says the church will adapt everything but its message, so long as that message gets through.

I believe that God is in the process of changing our ideas about his church. The evidence is all around us, and I will enumerate some of this evidence later. For now, we need to come to an understanding of three basic models of church life. Each of these paradigms has different rules about how many services should be held, who is allowed to preach, what musical styles are permissible, and how unity within the church is achieved. After exploring these three models, we will try to answer the question, "Do the differences matter?" To find an answer, we will take a brief look at systems analysis as it relates to churches.

The Paradigms

The Traditional Model

"Tradition" means different things to different people at different times. What I mean by "traditional" in this context is this: *One pastor preaching to one group, all together at the same time and place (usually Sunday morning at 11:00).* But the most traditional people at *our* church do not worship at 11:00 A.M. on Sundays. They attend at 8:30 A.M. Radical? Perhaps. I hope the next generation of churches will regard the multi-congregational model as "traditional." For many churches today the multi-service model falls in that category. The church may have a multiple staff, but only one preaching pastor. There may be a Sunday-evening service, or a mid-week service, but there is one *primary* service when the "whole church" is together.

This model has the advantage of unity. Everyone feels like part of the same group because they are all together every week with the same leader. It is one big happy family, whether there are 30 or 3,000 members, although very few actually grow that large.

Communication is simple. Announce something on Sunday morning and everyone gets the news. If you want to talk to someone at church, you do not have to worry about what service that person attends. You do not have the embarrassing experience of shaking hands with someone, introducing yourself, and asking, "Are you visiting with us today?" and having him or her respond, "No, I have been a member for two years. I attend on Saturday night."

Let me say up front that this is not a bad model, and these are not bad churches. In many contexts it is the best way of doing things. My brother-in-law pastors a church in a rural area of Colorado that is sparsely populated. Construction of the building they enjoy was a community project, Christian and non-Christian alike. It was a grand barn-raising event that the whole community celebrated. For these people, the traditional model makes sense, but in an urban setting, with a more diverse population and cost of land and construction out of sight, it is a growth-limiting model. Consequently, most growing churches employ other alternatives.

The Multi-Service Model

John Vaughan conducted a study revealing that 85 percent of growing churches are in what can be called a multi-service model.[4] *This type of church has two or more primary services per week.* Some of these churches do this by necessity and others because they prefer it that way. Even if they feel the church really ought to worship as one body, some may need to have multiple services temporarily, until larger facilities can be constructed. John Vaughan told me he would never recommend that a church construct another building until it was holding at least three primary services. (Services that people attend a second time in the week would not count as "primary.")

All these churches, however, will have a couple of other characteristics. First, they will have a secondary service, perhaps on Sunday evening or Wednesday evening, where "the whole church" meets together. I put that in quotes because it is not really the entire body, but only those people who wish to attend twice a week. This includes the leadership core of the church as well as the people who miss seeing each other on Sunday morning (because some come at 8:30 and others at 11:00). The secondary service is usually less formal and less seeker-oriented—it is a believers' service. This point of unity is very important to the multi-service church, but it also limits the number of times available for the primary service—because before long it will run out of space for this secondary service. If there are three Sunday-morning services needed, the Sunday-night or Wednesday-night service will soon be overcrowded.

The second characteristic that marks the multi-service church is that there will be only one preaching pastor. The stamina of this pastor will also limit the number of times the congregation can meet. How many times per week can you ask a pastor to preach? If you expect more than four times weekly, books on "burnout" will start to look really interesting, especially to the senior pastor. Our experience has confirmed what Bill Hybels recently told a New Community audience at Willow Creek (midweek believers' service): "It is no longer physically, emotionally, or spiritually possible for one individual to teach five times a week, every week, week in and week out. If he tries, it will destroy him."[5] It just can't be done. The senior pastor may be able to do the preaching, but he will not have the energy for the broad-based leadership that every church needs. When Benno Schmidt, Jr., assumed the presidency of Yale University, he expressed this need for leisure thinking time: "If I can't put my feet on the desk and look out the window and think without an agenda, I may be *managing* Yale, but I won't be *leading* it."[6] It is the same with pastors. They need uncluttered mental time and enough energy to dream. Requiring five services a week will rob the best of them of this. A pastor is the key to a myriad of nonpreaching church-related activities. If too much is expected of him, before long it will begin to wear. He will get up one Monday and say, "This is no longer rewarding work." The ministry will be a drag, so he will figure out something else to do. Lay church leaders should protect their pastor from this kind of discouragement. He loves you, he loves the Lord, and he loves to preach. But too much is like a bathtub full of strawberry shortcake—it will destroy his appetite and may even ruin his health.

The Multi-Congregation Model[7]

The multi-congregation model is now being explored by churches like Bear Valley in Denver, Willow Creek in Chicago, Dr. Cho's Central Church in Korea, and the church where I serve. Many of us feel intuitively that there is something very wasteful about using a building only once or twice a week, although we may not know exactly what it costs and cannot figure out anything different to do about it. Every other church we know is empty most of the time, too, but it does not seem quite right. Perhaps you have wandered into a deserted church building and thought, "What a shame for this space to go unused all week." You might even wonder whether a business could survive if its capital resources were used this little. This should cause you to reflect on the grace of God!

There *is* a better way. The multi-congregation church has a unique mind-set about itself. The big difference from the two other models is not schedule but self-perception. The question is not how many services a church has; it is how many services a church believes it *ought* to have. In the multi-congregation church, holding multiple services is not a necessity so much as a preference. And, because such a church wants more services than can be expected of one preacher, it enjoys the preaching ministries of more than one pastor. *A multi-congregation church is one that endorses multiple services (both seekers' services and believers' services) and has more than one preaching pastor.*

Some churches, like Bear Valley in Denver, also have multiple locations. Although most of the secondary locations are primarily ministry centers for street people, unwed mothers and other special-needs groups, preaching services are also held there. On a taped message, the pastor said he preached four times on Sunday, and none of these services was at the primary location. At that point in the life of his church, his presence was needed elsewhere. I once called Bear Valley and asked a spokesperson "How many preaching pastors do you have?" The pause told the whole story: "Uh—six, I think. Let's see, there is our senior pastor and...." That is the multi-congregation church. I also talked to a student at Denver Seminary who is an intern at Bear Valley. He said that the senior pastor rotated preaching with one other pastor at his location every other week. When I commented, "So you do not know who is going to preach from one week to the next?" he replied, "If you attended last week, you do. Whoever did not preach last week will preach this week." That is the multi-congregation church.

I am told that Dr. Cho's church has a slightly different approach. There are seven services each Sunday. In addition, the church has several overflow rooms where people watch the main service via closed-circuit television. Here you do not know and cannot find out who will be preaching at which service on any particular day.

Another example of a church that followed the multi-congregation model is the Jerusalem church as described in the Book of Acts. This "church" had meetings every day and did not have buildings at all (more on this special example in chapter 3).

In a multi-congregation church, there is always the possibility of developing the Corinthian problem, wherein some say "I follow Paul," and others say, "I follow Apollos [or Cephas]" (see 1 Cor. 1:11–12). But if the preaching pastors are all equally competent and faithfully "follow" *Christ*, there is also a great advantage here. The body can benefit from the preaching gifts of more than one person.

I received my theological training from two different schools, one a very small school with three full-time professors in the religion department, and the other the world's largest—Southwestern Baptist Theological Seminary. Although I enjoyed them both, the learning experience was more diverse at the large school. In the smaller school, Wayland Baptist University, I soon felt that I had heard everything these men had to say. We students knew their jokes so well, we could mouth a punch line before it came out of a professor's mouth. And it was not just the jokes. We could predict a teacher's answer to almost any question—and predictability is the great destroyer of learning.

Things were far different at Southwestern, where there were dozens and dozens of truly great teachers. It was a privilege to learn from these brilliant and godly men. What a richness was gained from the variety of their experience and knowledge! My only regret was that I could not take more classes with them.

For the same reason, I love listening to preaching tapes. Among my favorites are Bill Hybels, John MacArthur, Rick Warren, R. C. Sproul, Chuck Smith, Joel Gregory, and Chuck Swindoll. What a shame, what a bore, if I had to listen to only one of these men. One of the advantages of the multi-congregation approach is the opportunity to hear Paul *and* Cephas *and* Apollos.

Do the Differences Matter?

"So what?" you might ask. What difference does it make? Is it not just a matter of personal preference on the part of a church as to which model it will adopt? Is this an issue of right and wrong or good and bad? Or is it just an "innocent" choice, just as some people like orange juice with breakfast and others prefer grapefruit? To answer this question, we need a brief primer on systems analysis.

Everything I know about systems, I learned from Peter Senge in the book, *The Fifth Discipline.*[8] Fascinating reading. An analogy will make it clear why this approach sheds so much light on the wisdom of choosing one model over another.

Consider a booming new computer company that is enjoying what Senge calls self-reinforcing cycles. Sales are up, which motivates the sales force to sell more products. The company has a great reputation, which encourages the public to buy. Up and up production levels rise. As the product recognition of the company improves further, sales go up even more. On and on goes the cycle. You would think that at this rate of growth, the company will dominate the market in ten years—just like a pastor who says, "We had four kids in our youth group three weeks ago, ten two weeks ago, and twenty last week. I predict that at this rate of growth we will have attracted all the city's young people in five years."

Then something else happens. A second cycle is driven by the first one, but it cannot keep up. Manufacturing output lags behind demand. Products that used to have a thirty-day delivery time now take twice as long or even longer. The pressures created by the high sales volume will eventually slow down the selling cycle, as disappointed customers lose confidence in the company's ability to fill their orders on time. Gross income falls, as may also the profit margin, since it is based on high volume.

The temptation at this point is to blame the sales force and not see that the system itself is flawed. Company executives try to pep up the sales people, but sales will never reach the projected goals until the manufacturing problem is solved and delivery time is thereby reduced. Of course, the problem will correct itself. Before long, sales will drop enough so that manufacturing can again match demand. Then we might expect that sales would begin to pick up again, but reputation is a company's most important asset: "A good name is more desirable than great riches; to be esteemed is better than silver or gold" (Prov. 22:1). On the other hand, Proverbs 25:10 warns that if you betray another man's confidence, "you will never lose your bad reputation." What does this have to do with selling computers? Just this: A reputation for too-long delivery time is hard to break. Even after the problem is fixed, the company may not be able to regain their market share. What is the solution?

Only a systems view can provide the answer. Strange as it seems, what the company should do is raise prices slightly. This will do two things. It will temporarily slow sales until manufacturing can keep up. It will also increase profitability so that expanded facilities can be built sooner than expected. This path will result in steady growth, provided it is taken before the company's good name is damaged beyond repair.

What does this have to do with growing churches? For one thing, *reputation* is at stake. Churches that raise money for a building that will be used only once a week will turn off many of the very people they are trying to reach. And churches that attempt bigger projects than they can reasonably accomplish will run into the same sort of thing, just as a weightlifter who attempts to lift too much weight may strain a muscle and then not be able to lift at all. Because muscles heal, that problem is self-correcting, if the athlete has learned his lesson. The outcome may be less favorable when a *church* is trying to lift too heavy a load. At the old rate of growth, the new building might be adequate, but the building process itself will kill the growth of the church. There will come a day when some will wonder if they needed the new building at all. I know of a pastor who, because of financial pressure from the lay leadership, was forced to make impassioned appeals for money during the Christmas Eve service. The church had a payment due on the first. The bad reputation earned during those days will be very hard to lose. The Bible tells me so.

It is not that people are not generous or that every building-fund promotion is ill-conceived or poorly executed. Sometimes we blame the sales force: People are not witnessing enough. Or we blame the CEO: The pastor is an ineffective motivator. But the system itself is flawed! Until the system is fixed, we tend to blame the wrong people. Discovering that it is no one's fault is what systems analysis is all about.

When parking space is limited, all the witnessing training in the world will not grow a church. When preschool facilities are shabby and dimly lit, or inadequate care is given, praying alone will not pull a church out of a membership slump. We will never reach people without prayer, but the delivery system has an impact on our results. When we share with nonbelievers and they receive Christ, will not the church grow despite its limited parking? Not necessarily, as the following example will show.

Chill Out!

Peter Senge calls this the Beer Game, but I will call it the Chill Game. "Chill" is a fictional soda pop. Through computer simulation, three players enter a distribution chain. Player One owns Sleepy's, a convenience store in Riverfront, U.S.A. Player Two drives a truck and helps manage a warehouse for all kinds of soft drinks. Player Three runs the Chill Soda Company. Week in and week out, things down at Sleepy's are predictable. Joe Bob, the store owner, does not see any new faces, does not sell more than two cases of Chill, and does not take American Express. He has been ordering two cases a week for so long, he does not even remember the last time he counted the eight cases he keeps in stock. The ordering *system* works like this: Joe Bob fills out an order form and hands it to the truck driver, who attaches it to a stack of other orders on a clipboard. Joe's order arrives back at the warehouse at the end of the driver's weekly run. Two weeks are spent in processing this order, as the manager verifies Joe Bob's credit history and reconciles all the incoming orders with the distribution center's supply. Delivery takes another week. By the time Joe Bob gets his order, he is receiving cases of Chill that he actually ordered a month ago. There is a similar ordering system and time lag in delivery between the Chill plant and the distributor. This does not bother Joe Bob. In the sleepy town called Riverfront not much bothers anyone. If someone gets bothered, Joe Bob will hand him a soda and say, "Read the label." All is well at Riverfront.

Along comes an effective new ad that jumps sales volume on Chill from two cases a week to four cases a week. Watch the effect ripple through the *system*. Joe Bob does not notice the increase the first week because he has not been counting his stock. The second week he notices he has no cases in reserve, but he does not do anything until the third week, when he runs out of Chill. Although he doubles his order, he runs out of Chill again. The next week his usual order of two cases comes in. He sells them in two days and wonders if he should have ordered more than the four cases that won't be delivered for another three weeks. He steps his order up to six cases, just to be sure. The next week two cases arrive, as expected, but Joe Bob is getting a little ticked. He sells his two cases in two days again and orders ten more, just to be sure. When Joe Bob calculates the sales loss over the past three weeks due to his inability to meet the demand, he decides to take the bull by the horns and order sixteen cases. One more week of this and he is up to ordering twenty-four cases. Finally, the first order of four cases arrives. He barely gets through the week and continues to place large orders so he can build his stock back up to eight cases. Even when he has a surplus of two cases, he is still worried, so he orders twenty-four more.

Let me get to the point. Joe Bob eventually has nearly a hundred cases of Chill. At four cases a week, it will take him a year to sell it off—except that the ad campaign has been canceled, and sales are heading back toward two cases a week. When the bills for these extra hundred cases come in, it becomes difficult for Joe Bob to chill out! The same thing happens at the warehouse. They slowly start getting larger orders and then peak out with huge orders they cannot fill. They put them on back order, which explains why it took even longer than expected for the larger orders to be filled. Joe Bob did not cause the problem. Neither did the distributor. They were just part of the system. And the system was flawed. By the time the big shipments got to Joe Bob, he did not need them. By the time the big shipments came to the warehouse from the plant, the distributor did not need them anymore. Sales to retail outlets had begun to plummet. Depending on the way the computer simulation players react, the disaster reaches various proportions, but there is always a disaster when the *system* is flawed. Smart business minds can play this game and not do much better than novices. The system is at fault.

Several lessons can be learned from this systems analogy. Notice that the Chill delivery system included a delay, just as there was a delay before the new computer factory could be built. But by the time the expanded facility was built, the problem was irrevocable. The customer was lost. The system is flawed.

Our churches, too, need to reevaluate their delivery system. When Christian leaders have to stand before their people and berate them for not witnessing, it is evidence of a faulty system. Of course, Christians ought to witness. But when you have to nag people constantly about their moral obligation to do something that ought to be the most natural, obvious thing in the world to do, I say we should look carefully at the system. Some things ought to be obvious. Maybe then we can discover why the Good News is not being delivered efficiently by the modern church, and why there are so many "dissatisfied customers."

Early in this century, missionary thinker Roland Allen was making this very same point:

> When we turn from the restless entreaties and exhortations which fill the pages of our modern missionary magazines to the pages of the New Testament, we are astonished at the change in the atmosphere. St. Paul does not repeatedly exhort his churches to subscribe money for the propagation of the Faith, he is far more concerned to explain to them what the Faith is, and how they ought to practice it and to

keep it. The same is true of St. Peter and St. John, and of all the apostolic writers. They do not seem to feel any necessity to repeat the Great Commission and to urge that it is the duty of their converts to make disciples of all nations. What we do read in the New Testament is no anxious appeal to Christians to spread the gospel, but a note here and there which suggests how the gospel was being spread abroad: "the churches were established in the Faith, and increased in number daily."[9]

I am going to argue that part of the problem relates to our emphasis on buildings and related costs. There are too many delays in the system. It might not seem like the size of our buildings and the number of times we use them would have anything to do with whether we are motivated to share our faith. We tend not to see those factors as part of the "distribution chain," but they are.

If you place twenty four-year-olds in a room designed for ten, you are going to have discipline problems. You may characterize the kids as delinquent, rotten, and poorly behaved. You may blame the parents for being too lenient, or the teacher for being ill-prepared. (She may blame *herself* and quit.) The kids may not be angels, the parents may not be perfect, and the teacher could probably improve her skills. But, if you gave her a bigger room and a helper or two, or you divided the class, you would be surprised how much that would fix. The system needs to be improved.

If McDonald's built restaurants so large that only 10 percent of the capacity was ever filled, they would fail. Quality hamburgers, competitive prices, attractive facilities, friendly, trained personnel, and cutting-edge management techniques at Hamburger University could never overcome a system that invested ten times what was really necessary in capital expenditures.

Churches could cut their capital expenditures by 90 percent if they met ten times as often. This is the multi-congregation approach, and it does make a difference—because it improves the system. It is not only less expensive, it works better because it allows a church to provide more choices. This is how the early church operated. It is our primary model of church life in the New Testament. It is not new and different; it returns to the original approach. Of course, the early churches did not have buildings, so there was a zero on that line of the budget. They didn't start building programs for 250 years—about when their skyrocketing growth began to level off!

What Systems Cannot Do

Some who read this will get the mistaken notion that with the proper systems we can do anything—with or without God. Those of us who have dabbled in marketing, business, and advertising have to constantly guard our hearts against this kind of thinking. We are tempted to believe in throwing big stacks of money toward advertising, having a slick music program, and perhaps taking a multi-media approach. So we include some Bill Hybels-style messages and make sure the music is contemporary and the whole style is "in." We learn our demographics, sharpen our marketing savvy, and expect that "Bingo!" the whole thing will be done. We also pray, of course. But I don't think there are many things more distasteful to God than people who try to do his work in the power of the flesh. God seeks first a relationship with us, to know us as sons and daughters. He wants us to abide in him on a daily basis. He wants us to follow him in what *he* is doing, not consult a carefully worked-out pro forma.

Good systems cannot produce repentance and faith. They do not cause people to pray well, love their families, and lead lives of holiness. They do not cause people to enjoy God. The best of systems will not guarantee a spiritual harvest. But a faulty system can work against the progress of the kingdom.

Examine your heart. Jesus said that apart from him we can produce nothing of true, lasting value (John 15:5). I would like to think I can do quite a bit, and somewhat better if I abide in Christ. But Jesus said that is not the case: Without him I can do *nothing*. Henry Blackaby rightly warns that churches are often guilty of a copy-cat mentality that only wants to mimic what another church has done.[10] We do far better if we get alone with God and follow him in what he is doing in our place and time.

Even more important than the system is following God.

3

Is the Everyday Church Biblical?

Even a casual reading of the Book of Acts will uncover several references to early Christians as meeting every day. As I will demonstrate in this chapter, this is almost certain proof that the first "churches" were multi-congregational, not traditional in the sense of having one pastor and one body of members meeting once a week. It is not my purpose to persuade you that this is normative or the only right pattern, but only that it is allowable. If the early church met every day, it is all right for us to meet every day. In another chapter we will examine some of the practical advantages of the everyday church that could make us more effective in fulfilling the Great Commission. I think you would agree that if a certain system is allowed by Scripture and would also improve on how we spread the gospel, the burden of proof shifts to the other side. We are forced to ask, "Why not?" and come up with compelling answers to that question. It may be that this was *the* New Testament pattern, but it is not my purpose here to prove that.

New Testament "Evidence"

As an introduction, I would simply like to place before you the New Testament texts that relate to this subject. I will be citing both the ones that support the everyday—hence multi-congregation view—and those that could be used to support the idea that *Sunday* is the primary day appropriate for rest and worship. Honest research demands that I present both sides. (I have added italics to emphasize the points in question.)

The verses that have been used to support the idea that Sunday is the primary day for Christian worship are:

> *"On the first day of the week we came together to break bread.* Paul spoke to the people and, because he intended to leave the next day, kept on talking until midnight"* (Acts 20:7).
>
> *"On the first day of every week,* each one of you should set aside a sum of money in keeping with his income, saving it up, so that when I come no collections will have to be made" (1 Cor. 16:2).
>
> *"On the Lord's Day* I was in the Spirit, and I heard behind me a loud voice like a trumpet" (Rev. 1:10).

Three verses state directly that the early church did not come together once or twice a week but met every single day:

> *"Every day* they continued to meet together in the temple courts. They broke bread in their homes and ate together with glad and sincere hearts" (Acts 2:46).
>
> *"Day after day,* in the temple courts and from house to house, they never stopped teaching and proclaiming the good news that Jesus is the Christ" (Acts 5:42).

"But some of them became obstinate; they refused to believe and publicly maligned the Way. So Paul left them. He took the disciples with him and had discussions *daily* in the lecture hall of Tyrannus" (Acts 19:9).

Other verses, though not dealing with the subject directly, imply an everyday meeting of the church:

"Praising God and enjoying the favor of all the people. And the Lord added to their number *daily* those who were being saved" (Acts 2:47).
"So the churches were strengthened in the faith and grew *daily* in numbers" (Acts 16:5).
"Now the Bereans were of more noble character than the Thessalonians, for they received the message with great eagerness and examined the Scriptures *every day* to see if what Paul said was true" (Acts 17:11).
"But *encourage one another daily,* as long as it is called Today, so that none of you may be hardened by sin's deceitfulness" (Heb. 3:13).

It may be that the question arose early in the life of the church as to whether they should keep meeting every day or set aside one day for worship. The preferred day from our records of the early church fathers is clearly Sunday rather than the Sabbath.[1] This explains certain of Paul's admonitions:

"One man considers one day more sacred than another; another man considers *every day alike.* Each one should be fully convinced in his own mind" (Rom. 14:5).
"But now that you know God—or rather are known by God—how is it that you are turning back to those weak and miserable principles? Do you wish to be enslaved

by them all over again? *You are observing special days and months and seasons and years?"* (Gal. 4:9–10). "Therefore do not let anyone judge you by what you eat or drink, or with regard to a religious festival, a New Moon celebration or *a Sabbath day.* These are a shadow of the things that were to come; the reality, however, is found in Christ" (Col. 2:16–17).

In light of these verses, it would be difficult to see how any thinking person could arrive at the conclusion that the everyday church is not allowed by Scripture. Paul is clearly saying that it is acceptable to "consider every day alike." Apparently there were Christians in Rome who believed neither in Sabbath worship, nor in Sunday worship, but in everyday worship, and Paul commended them for it.

I turn now to a brief discussion of each of these verses.

References to Sunday as the Day of Worship (Acts 20:7; 1 Cor. 16:2; Rev. 1:10)

John Scott, in his defense of Sunday-only worship, uses Acts 20:17 as a primary text supporting his view.[2] Well he should, for there are only three New Testament references, direct or indirect, to Sunday-only worship. But a closer look at the text reveals a number of things that cannot be considered normative for all churches everywhere. The text says that *this particular meeting* was "on the first day of the week," not that every church everywhere for all times should take this as the norm. Similarly, other verses speak of people speaking in tongues after they receive the Holy Spirit, but Paul is clear that this is not expected to happen to everyone. The text also says that this meeting lasted until midnight, but we do not adopt that as a normative part of church life. (Our people are grateful for that!) Much of the Book of Acts describes particular events, rather than sets norms for the church then or now. The passages that speak of the church as meeting every day are much more general than Acts 20:7, which is describing one solitary meeting. This is a rather weak foundation on which to build a Sunday-only doctrine, especially when pitted against the verses dealing with an everyday church.

It is clear not only from the New Testament itself, but from the unanimous voice of the Fathers, that the church early on moved to Sunday as the primary day of worship. There was never much controversy about this. Where there was controversy, it centered around the Sabbath question— whether the church should meet on Sunday or on Saturday. Apparently, the question of everyday worship was not discussed. However, honest scholars recognize that the Sunday-worship view is not a settled question. D. K. Lowery says, "That the practice of the early church customarily met on Sunday during the New Testament era cannot be unequivocally demonstrated."[3] Donald Guthrie admits, "At first it [worship] seems to have been on a daily basis."[4] Gene Getz points out, "The Bible certainly does not dictate any patterns in this area [how many meetings and when]. There is little said in the New Testament about when the church met. Some would even question that meeting on Sunday is an absolute guideline for the church, but rather an example of when the church met."[5]

Direct References to the Everyday Church (Acts 2:46; 5:42; 19:9)

It is clear from these verses that the early church met every single day, even as late as Paul's ministry to Ephesus during his third missionary journey. One could argue that this was *the primary pattern* of the early church, but that is not my purpose here. Instead, let us examine what this meant for the church and its leaders, at least in Jerusalem.

First, they had two kinds of meetings: house to house and in the temple courts. Some would argue that this speaks against organizations like Sunday school that meet in facilities built for that purpose. I disagree—the point here is substance, not form. The central idea is that the early church had two kinds of meetings: large group/temple court/celebration-type meetings, and small group/in home/face-to-face meetings.

Second, consider the effect of everyday church meetings for average Christians living in Jerusalem. Would they attend a small-group and a large-group meeting every day? I do not think so. It is reasonable to assume that although there were meetings every day, the typical believer went to one or two of each type of meeting per week. Oh, there were probably a few hard-chargers who went more often, but there is no indication from the culture that the people had any more leisure time than we do. They probably had less, for it was an agrarian society that often worked men and women in the fields from daylight to dark with no long weekends. How could they have all met day after day and still cared for the needs of their families and the other demands of life? And the texts do not demand this interpretation. They simply say that the church, or part of it, was meeting every day in some fashion, not that every single believer came every single day to both a small-group and a large-group worship service.

Third, consider what this meant for the elders and other staff. Do you think Peter preached all those services? He probably preached a lot of them, but even Peter could not preach them all. Apparently the work load on the apostles was bearable for a while, but eventually they needed help. Acts 6 tells us that the Twelve ordained seven men to carry out a ministry to widows. This is clear indication that the early church thought in terms of more than one preaching pastor:

In those days when the number of disciples was increasing, the Grecian Jews among them complained against the Hebraic Jews because their widows were being overlooked in the daily distribution of food. So the Twelve gathered all the disciples together and said, "It would not be right for *us to neglect the ministry of the word of God* in order to wait on tables. . . . And [we] will give our attention to prayer and the ministry of the word." (Acts 6:1–2, 4, italics mine)

Not, "I will preach and the other guys will administer the program," but "*we* will give our attention to the preaching of the Word." The idea of having only one preaching pastor was foreign to the early church. A plurality of preaching elders, with one leader among them, was the norm. Peter was presumably the first among equals at this time. Later, the leadership of the Jerusalem church was passed to James, the brother of our Lord.[6] But, in the everyday church, the preaching must have been shared.

Indirect References to an Everyday Church (Acts 2:47; 16:5; 17:11; Heb. 3:13)

These verses tell us that several things were happening in the early church every day. It was growing in number *every day*. People were being saved *every day*. They were growing in faith *every day*. They were checking up on Paul's teaching *every day*. They were encouraging one another *every day*. It is possible that these things were taking place outside the confines of regular church meetings, but I doubt it. In light of the other clear references about the early church meeting every day, it makes more sense to conclude that all this happened within the context of regular church meetings, either in the home or in the temple courts. John R. W. Stott sees daily meetings in the Berean passage: "[They were] meeting Paul for a daily dialogue and not just a weekly one on the Sabbath."[7] If this is true, there are not three but seven direct or indirect references to an everyday church.

Furthermore, as was mentioned in discussing the Jerusalem church, I believe we can conclude that the idea of a plurality of preaching pastors, though foreign to the practice of most modern churches, clearly determined the pattern of the early church. This is so patently evident that it is hardly an issue of debate among scholars. Stott is a good example of this: "We notice [the form of pastoral oversight] was both local and plural—local in that the elders were chosen from within the congregation, not imposed from without, and plural in that the familiar modern pattern of 'one pastor one church' was simply unknown."[8] Does it not logically follow that the early church was multi-congregational?

How "Special" Is Sunday?
(Rom. 14:5; Gal. 4:9–10; Col. 2:16–17)

In the early church there arose a debate between those who felt every day was alike, those who hailed the Jewish Sabbath, and those who opted for Sunday as the day of worship. It is generally agreed by conservative scholars that the church gradually designated Sunday as the primary day of worship but stopped short of calling it the "Christian Sabbath." This is not to say that worshipping on Sunday is a "turning back" to a weak principle, a practice to be avoided, according to Paul in Galatians 4:9. The view that Sunday is the day of worship does not mean that we are being "enslaved" by Old Testament principles that violate the New Testament. Worshipping on Sunday is fine, but declaring that Sunday is the *only* available day for worship is quite another thing. The Sabbath, as well as all of the law, was fulfilled in Christ. The kind of stringent Sabbath legislation found in the Pentateuch is not mentioned in the New Testament with reference to Sunday. It therefore seems inappropriate for believers to be condemned for working on Sunday, even if that employment is not a necessity. If we are against people working on Sunday and want to be consistent in this matter, we should refrain from all goods and services that are delivered on Sunday. We cannot enjoy Sunday dinner at a restaurant and meanwhile look down our noses at those who are serving us as being "unspiritual" for working on that day. There is evidence, however, that the church adopted Sunday as a special day of worship fairly early in its history.

The significant thing here is that *both* views are supported by Paul. He is saying in these passages that if you want to have church services every day, go for it! Some modern writers disagree. Scott, for example, writes that Sunday is indeed "special":

> We are fast becoming a non-Christian nation, and we can mark its beginnings with the relaxation of rest and worship on the Lord's day. . . . For us to acquiesce to the pressures of our day, and to become a part of all the recreational activity that is now reserved for Sundays, is to *deny God's sovereignty* [emphasis added].[9]

J. I. Packer points out that the practice of showing extreme reverence for Sunday as a kind of Christian Sabbath dates back to the Puritans. They had one day a week that was market day, and it seemed convenient to have one day a week that was marked as worship day. On market day, all the people would bring their goods together and exchange products. We have a similar practice here in Las Cruces. Every Saturday the local farmers set up stands in a designated area and have a "farmers market." The local people know this is the best place to get fresh green chiles and other locally grown produce. It is also only available once a week, and that during the growing season. The Puritans patterned their worship schedule after this sort of arrangement. They set aside one day for worship, just as they had one day for merchandising.

Relevance for the Modern Church

The early church met every day. It was a multi-congregation church with a number of preaching pastors. The idea of having only one or two primary meeting times each week under the direction of one teacher was foreign to the early church. Does this prove that modern Christians should adopt this pattern of meeting?

No.

Even though this was the pattern of the early church, the New Testament does not demand that we organize ourselves that way. Here I am only arguing that it is *allowed.* Only if we can find compelling reasons to believe that following the multi-congregation approach would help us in fulfilling our God-given mission should we consider such a change. The next chapter will consider whether any such reasons can be found.

If the multi-congregational church is allowed by Scripture, and there are sound reasons to believe that it will help us fulfill the Great Commission, the only prudent course of action is to explore in depth the possibility of becoming a multi-congregation church on a permanent and *intentional* basis.

4

Advantages of the Multi-Congregation Model

It is my purpose in this chapter to demonstrate that a change toward a multi-congregational approach could have significant impact on the church and our ability to fulfill the Great Commission. If it is allowed by Scripture, which I have already shown, and would help us reach more persons for Christ, the conclusion seems obvious. As soldiers engaged in spiritual warfare, we must forgo our personal preferences in this matter. I set before you ten reasons why the multi-congregational approach is practically advantageous in terms of making disciples of all nations (Matt. 28:19).

1. It frees more resources and laborers for the harvest.

The money you spend on "a" cannot be spent on "b." My mother taught me this principle. When driving home from church on Sunday night, we often drove by McDonald's. If I asked to stop and get a hamburger instead of having something cooked at home, she would suggest that we use that money for a better purpose, reminding me that "the money you spend at McDonald's cannot also be spent for missions." Mom tells me she learned this principle from Winston Crawley when he was area director for Southeast Asia for the Southern Baptist Foreign Mission Board. (My parents were missionaries to the Philippines for twenty-five years.) If the missionaries suggested that they build an orphanage or other project, Crawley would always respond, "That is a good idea for a ministry. But, remember, the money you spend on an orphanage you cannot also spend on placing a church planter in a new area." We cannot spend the same dollar on buildings, staff, program expenses, and world missions.

A finite amount of resources is available to Christian ministry. There is a fine line between saying that God's resources are unlimited (which is true) and recognizing that the resources he releases for Christian ministry are limited (which is equally true). Some say, "If God wants it done, resources will not be a problem." Yes, God has promised to meet all our needs. However, we must candidly recognize that God, in his infinite wisdom, has seen it best not to give us a blank check, even for ministry. If this were not true, how could we justify not already having a full slate of staff at every church in America? Would it not help your church to have a minister for children, for youth, for music, for singles, for evangelism, and so on—a full-time shepherd for every needs group? Surely there is a need to reach as many people as possible, and additional equippers would help us get more accomplished. So why are the resources not available? Because God would have us make wise choices on where to spend our money.

If funds available for Christian ministry *were* unlimited, every church could spend money on a soup kitchen for the poor, a home for unwed mothers, centers for drug rehabilitation, and a host of other social ministries. Budget planning would be unnecessary if we could wave a magic wand to get what we want. But, because resources are limited, many worthy causes must be left undone. Nevertheless, churches should always be eager to hire as many workers as is fiscally responsible, supplementing this labor pool with a dedicated group of volunteers.

God would have us invest our resources in the wisest way to produce the maximum results. Every church has its own unique statement of purpose. We have defined the purpose of our church as "to glorify God by making disciples of Jesus Christ. This will result in helping people live better lives." If building a large-enough complex so that the whole membership can gather together every week will help your church fulfill its purpose, go ahead and pour a big slab. But realize that you cannot have it all. If you pour that slab, you may not be able to hire that children's minister you need. The question, then, is which will best fulfill your central purpose?

Available resources can be predicted. Each man, woman, and child who walks through the door and sits down in a Sunday-school class drops about $22.00 in the offering plate every time he or she comes. At least that has been the average for many years across the Southern Baptist Convention.[1] I do not have numbers for other denominations, but I suspect they are about the same. This is really fairly generous. We complain about spending five dollars to go to a movie, yet most people willingly give at least four times as much to the church each week. Note that this is based on Sunday school attendance. Churches that do not depend on the Sunday school as their primary small-group system will have to come up with a different means of calculating. However, the point is the same: Resources available for Christian ministry can be predicted. It is reasonable to assume that these figures represent the approximate amount of resources that God will make available to his people to do his work. (Perhaps we should say that these are the resources God's people are *choosing* to make available.) Because giving is tied to attendance, we can predict, with a fair degree of accuracy the level of available funding.

Major expenses can be predicted. A predictable number of square feet is needed to provide worship and education space for a given number of people. Lyle Schaller observes, "Experience tells us the answer [to the question, "What will it cost?"] will turn out to be two or three or four times the original estimate."[2] The amount of space needed for education varies according to age groups. Children require more space than adults. Taken as a whole, we need about ten square feet of space per person in the auditorium or sanctuary and forty square feet for education. (This includes classrooms, hallways, rest rooms, offices, and storage.) Churches that utilize home groups rather than a fully graded Sunday school are at a cost advantage here, but the latter is probably the best way to provide a quality small group educational experience for a multi-age family. In other words, under one roof, we can provide a positive small-group experience for the adults, youth activities for the teenagers, education for the grade-schoolers, and actual teaching (not baby-sitting) for the preschoolers. (See chapter 9 section, "Make Decisions About Sunday School," for more on this.) We do not wish to argue with those who want to go the home-group route, but our church feels this is how God has called us. As Rick Warren comments in his Church Growth Seminar, it takes all kinds of churches to reach all kinds of people.

But this kind of care comes at a price. At a cost of $50 per square foot, this means a church would need to spend $2,500 per person on construction, in addition to the cost of the land. Land costs vary widely, but if we figure $75,000 per acre[3] and 150 people per acre, this would add an additional $500 per person for real estate, which does not include parking costs. If this were amortized for 30 years,

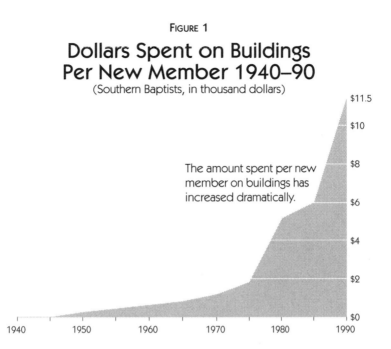

FIGURE 1

Dollars Spent on Buildings
Per New Member 1940–90
(Southern Baptists, in thousand dollars)

The amount spent per new member on buildings has increased dramatically.

$11.5
$10
$8
$6
$4
$2
$0

1940   1950   1960   1970   1980   1990

the monthly bill for providing space for 100 people would be about $3,000. (Paying the loan off in less than 30 years would raise the monthly payments correspondingly.) The total expected income from these same 100 people is less than $10,000 per month. Remember, this is *total* income, so it must cover salaries, maintenance, and other fixed expenses, as well as benevolences. It is every dollar that we can expect to be dropped into the offering plate. Some churches might do a little better, but chances are that your church will not differ greatly from the national average. This means that taken as a whole, the traditional model could spend as much as 25 to 33 percent of its income on capital expenses, i.e., buildings. Each time we add a service, we reduce the proportional amount spent on buildings.

The cost of physical facilities is going out of sight! Figure 1 shows the skyrocketing price of providing space for South-

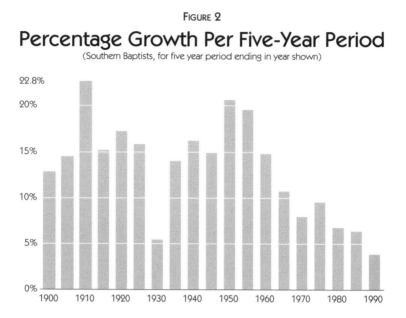

FIGURE 2

Percentage Growth Per Five-Year Period

(Southern Baptists, for five year period ending in year shown)

ern Baptists. In 1955 we spent $486.20 for every new member we added. In 1988 the figure was $12,057.64. This is an increase of a factor of twenty-five. Yet per capita giving (based on membership) grew from $39.51 to $278.66, only a sevenfold increase.

George Barna comments, "The average church in America allocates about 5 percent of its budget for evangelism, but approximately *30 percent for buildings and maintenance.* Another study reported the American Church as a whole spending $3 *billion* per year on the construction of new buildings" [emphasis added].[4]

What has happened to growth during this same period? Has this increase in costs hurt us? You be the judge—take a look at figure 2.

Airlines know they have tremendous capital invested in their planes, but the only time they are producing a profit is when those planes are in the air and full of people. Similarly, churches have huge resources tied up in their buildings, but the only time they are producing disciples is when they are occupied. The more often we fill those buildings, the wiser we have been in caring for the resources that God has entrusted to us as stewards. A church's bottom line is not dollars; it is people.

Looking at the overall picture, we are startled by the facts. In 1988 the average church with 500 in worship spent $187,000 on new construction. Churches in general average an indebtedness of an amount equal to 45 percent of their annual budget.[5] Leith Anderson warns that churches are spending five times as much on buildings and maintenance as they do on promoting evangelism.[6] Southern Baptists have invested $6,000 overall in buildings for every man, woman, and preschooler who attends their Sunday schools.[7]

More bad news: The revenue for this $6,000 per person does not come in evenly. Roughly 80 percent of it comes from 20 percent of the congregation, which means leaders are paying out $24,000 per person. If you sit on the elder board or session or if you are a deacon or Sunday-school teacher who has been asked to consider the multi-congregation model for your church, you will want to give sober attention to the high cost of supporting a traditional ministry. In fact, Ralph Neighbor says, using the traditional model will almost certainly terminate the growth of the church: "Since their activities are extremely building-centered, they choke off growth by growing large enough that they can no longer afford to add further space to their facilities. Few options remain for the American church."[8]

For some, this may seem too crass an approach. Are we not commissioned to further the kingdom at any cost—to trust that God will provide whatever we need to accomplish his purposes? However, Jesus taught that he who is "faithful with a few things" will be put in charge of "many things" (Matt. 25:21). He meant that if we are not faithful in handling worldly wealth, he will not entrust us with spiritual riches. Obviously, unless the Spirit of God moves, people will not be drawn unto God. But we need to be careful not to assume that every problem is a spiritual one. If parking or interior space is limited, attendance will be limited, too. Praying for the harvest is important, but so is providing enough room for those who hunger for its blessings.

The bottleneck in the evangelistic process is caused by unwise utilization of workers. Jesus said: "The harvest is plentiful, but the workers are few. Ask the Lord of the harvest, therefore, to send out workers into his harvest field" (Luke 10:2).

After spending years laboring toward the harvest, Dawson Trotman asked:

What is the need of the hour? For a beggar on the street it's a dime. For a woman going to the hospital it's a doctor. In Christian work we often feel the need is a larger staff. Many a minister would like to have an assistant. Better facilities and equipment. A training center. Communications—radio, literature.

Some think they need more time. Or money, the biggest of all needs. Frankly, I don't believe the need of the hour is any of these. . . . I believe the need of the hour is an army of soldiers dedicated to serve Jesus Christ in getting the Gospel to every creature—who believe not only that He's God, but that He can fulfill every promise He has ever made, and that there isn't anything too hard for Him.[9]

The bottleneck has always been laborers. The world is more willing to listen than the church is willing to send spokespeople.

In light of this I was surprised to learn that laborers are *not* in short supply! Dr. Russell Dilday, president of the Southwestern Baptist Theological Seminary in Fort Worth, Texas, said in a message several years ago that there are more ministers coming into the system than leaving. In fact, he pointed out there are about five hundred more ministers graduating from Southern Baptist seminaries than there are jobs opening up through ministers retiring, dying, or dropping out of the ministry, and new churches being planted. Why are churches not hiring these people? Why are trained, committed, available laborers not being placed on church staffs to provide evangelism, administration, and other needed ministries?

In a word, *money.*

And this is not just in my denomination. Peter Wagner reminds us: "One of the severe problems that many of the traditional denominations have been facing is a *surplus* of ordained clergy" [emphasis added].[10] He cites a major study done by Jackson Carroll and Robert Wilson and publicized in a book entitled *Too Many Pastors?*[11] This is a curious title in light of Jesus' teaching on the need for laborers in the harvest field.

Most churches would love to hire additional staff if they could afford it. Would not God want us to use the multi-congregation model if it could relieve the bottleneck in the labor supply—releasing financial resources so more full-time ministers could be bringing in the harvest?

The more money we can release toward laborers in the field, the more effective we will be in bringing in the harvest. There is an old rule that says if you want to have 1,000 in Sunday school, just get 100 teachers. And each of them will bring in 10 pupils. On a broader scale, if you want to increase the size of the harvest, add more full-time laborers in the field. Sounds simple, but there are practical limitations.

I once had a conversation with some members of our personnel committee about future staff positions. (This was before we considered the multi-congregational approach and were saturating our building in existing services.) Their unanimous and strongly held conviction was that we could not think about *any* new staff positions until after we had a new building. The choice was seen as between the two—one or the other. They understood instinctively that the money spent on "a," cannot be spent on "b." I agree that this viewpoint makes sense; the argument is compelling *if* you are committed to following the traditional model.

But there is a better way.

Schaller says, "A third common pitfall [of building campaigns] is to pay for new buildings out of salaries not paid to additional program staff who are not hired as part of an economy move. The result may be *very attractive but empty buildings* [emphasis added]."[12] Ted Engstrom writes, "We must continue to face the truth that churches . . . fail when they become prisoners of their buildings."[13] John Vaughan points out, "Once existing facilities of a church become strained, a crisis point in continued growth has already occurred. Members and potential members often have already been lost before this point is reached."[14]

Buildings are important and necessary. We need them. However, we need to think more clearly about this. Money spent on new buildings cannot be spent to pay the salary of equippers of ministry, but each time we *multiply* the use of our existing buildings, we release money that otherwise would have been required for construction costs.

This efficiency will have the side benefit of improving our image in the community at large. The world will notice us. For one thing, the sheer uniqueness of the multi-congregation church will draw people's attention. The frugality of it will impress them even more. We will not have to talk as often about what offends them the most: money. One of the objections by outsiders is that the institutional church seems not to really care about people; what it seems to do most is ask them for money for buildings used once a week.

2. It allows us to overcome the number-one obstacle facing the people we are trying to reach: inconvenience.

Rick Warren cites a major study done by Chrysler Corporation. The study discovered that the main thing Americans will not put up with is inconvenience. Once again, we can use an airlines analogy. An important watchword is again, "We are ready when you are." Dozens of flights are made daily between the same locations. In contrast, a church says, "We offer the life-saving message of the gospel on Sunday mornings [usually at 11:00]. If you are not available then, too bad. Apparently it is not important enough to you." Obviously, no church leader consciously feels this way, but that's what the outsider hears. Carl George is insightful at this point: "We have a custom for worship on Sunday, but for an increasing part of our population that is not working. Why can't we have worship sometime besides just Sunday? We don't think in those terms. We think of a worship service, or two worship services, and then we run out of imagination."[15]

A member of our congregation is a nurse. Although she gives high priority to her family, she finds it necessary to work outside the home to help with living expenses. Because of her commitment to her role as wife and mother, she decided to take a job where she could work twenty-four hours during the weekend and get paid for forty. While she is at work, her husband cares for their children, and they can all spend the rest of the week as a "normal" family. What would the traditional or even multi-service church have to offer this mother if it only had services on Sunday? Zilch. Many churches are just not available to people with such schedules. If we believe, as I do, that corporate worship is important, it is also important that we provide worship opportunities as many times as possible. The multi-congregation church can most effectively accomplish this. I once told a lady who visited our church about the many services we offer. She responded, "Well, there just isn't much excuse to stay away from church, is there?" You got it!

3. It makes it feasible to spend money on advertising.

A church will find it profitable to spend at least 5 percent of its income on advertising. (The retail clothing industry spends about that percentage.) The key is freeing-up the cash. The multi-congregation model, by reducing per-member overhead, can realize significant cash savings.

All the media can be used, but direct mail is probably the most predictable in terms of results. *Direct mail is the most cost-effective method of new-member enlistment available to churches.*[16] Experts tell us that for every batch of high-quality and creative mail dropped in local mailboxes, a church can expect to see .05 to 3 percent of those neighbors try the church.[17] In our experience, about a third of those who visit will join, and half of the new members will regularly attend. Total annual receipts will increase by at least $1,000 for every person attending.

Direct-mail campaigns can be done for about $.15 per piece, including printing, preparing a mailing list, postage, and processing.[18] A 10,000-piece mailing might cost $1,500. You can expect 50 to 300 people to visit as a result of that expenditure. If 54 visit, 18 will join. They will increase your attendance totals by an average of 9 and will contribute $9,000 their first year—not a bad return on your investment!

Of course, money is not all that is at stake here. Churches are in the people business. Even if the $1,500 were an out-right expense that we never expected to get back, it is always a joy to touch lives with the gospel and have new people join the church, some of them by conversion. But if we have to provide extra space for these people (at costs ranging from $3,000 to $6,000 each), the cash-flow problems become prohibitive. Part of the money the new members give will have to be spent on staff, program expenses, utilities, mission causes, and so on. Only if we can control capital expenses will advertising be affordable. If we don't have the money, because it is tied up in buildings, we simply lose this opportunity. The multi-congregation church makes better use of its physical facilities.

Americans are suspicious of messages they have not seen reinforced in the media. Although advertising is supplemental to word-of-mouth, it has a reinforcing effect that strengthens everything else we do. Committed Christians, living out the Christian walk and trying to witness as best they can, will always be our best advertising, but the media can reinforce this work.

I personally call many of the people who visit our church. One of the questions I ask is, "How did you hear of Calvary?" The usual response is, "Well, I work with someone at Calvary, *and* I also got this flyer in the mail." It took both incentives to get that person to church. Meeting a need will encourage a return visit.

I saved the best for last: Many of the people we touch through advertising come from the pagan pool. They have friends who are unbelievers and will invite them—if their own lives are changed. These are fringe people, but each time advertising attracts one of them, we are put in contact with a whole network of possible converts. This is why Schaller laments the failure to use direct-mail advertising to invite outsiders to special events and programs. "Very few long-established congregations are willing to affirm that spending an amount equivalent to as little as 5 percent of the annual budget is a cost-effective component of their growth strategy."[19]

4. It allows us to give more money to missions.

Because of its substantial savings on capital expenses, the multi-congregation church would be able to give more of its money to the cause of Christ, especially to foreign missions. It is beyond the scope of this book to delineate the enormous need for American churches to send missionaries and dollars overseas so as to reach the staggering number of spiritually hungry people around the world. Anything we can do to build a better pipeline to these people is worthy of careful consideration. The multi-congregational approach can broaden our global outreach, if only indirectly.

5. It recognizes that variety is the spice of life.

Not only is the multi-congregational approach cost-efficient in many ways, it recognizes the proven marketing strategy of going after specific target groups. It takes all kinds of churches to reach all kinds of people. The more hooks you cast in the water, and the more varied the bait, the more fish you will catch.

A multi-congregation church will offer many styles of preaching and a great variety of services. It makes use of the science of demographics, acknowledging the different needs, interests, and backgrounds of the population within its surrounding area, providing something to attract as many groups as possible. For example, it might have a ministry to singles, to young marrieds, to seniors, to teenagers, and even to a particular ethnic group in the community at large. Variety corners a market, whether the product being sold is ice cream, magazines, or the gospel.

Robert Tucker punches this point home when he says that our society is increasingly demanding more and more choices in everything it consumes. Toothpaste now comes in 138 different varieties; car buyers can choose from 572 makes and models; buying sneakers affords 1,000 styles to pick from; the IBM PC has over 30,000 different software programs. And the list goes on.[20] There is one noticeable exception, the traditional church that offers only one style of ministry and (usually) only one or two worship services.

Specialization of ministry would be no small advantage. Leith Anderson points out that one of the reasons we have not been more effective evangelistically is that we have failed to target specialized audiences with personalized messages.[21]

In our church, there was a marked increase in college-student attendance the year we added a 9:45 A.M. Sunday service. The young people were able to tell their friends, "Come to Calvary. They have a service just for us." How much more powerful it would be if every group could say the same thing.

As we try to become all things to all men, we will reach individuals more effectively. Schaller says, "In a growing number of churches with two [preaching] members on staff, the range of choices is expanded by scheduling different preachers for the two services."[22] He goes on to point out that this is such an advantage that even for churches that have more seating than they need, it would be better to decrease the number of seats and go to two services than to stay in one service with only one choice offered.[23] If two is better than one, why wouldn't ten or fifteen be better than two?

Radio stations have long recognized that specialization is necessary for survival. Imagine the folly of a station that broadcast a country song, followed by a rock song, followed by an "easy listening" song, followed by ten minutes of talk radio. People know what they want and when they want it. "A little bit of everything for everybody" might work in Small Town, USA (sometimes), but it will not work in Suburbia or metropolitan areas. The "little bit of everything" sounds good until everybody shows up and no one really likes anything. At best, we keep everyone equally dissatisfied.

Let me be quite candid: I hate country music. (Please don't quit reading; pray for me.) I am sorry, but the sound of the Grand Ole Opry is bad news to me. Give me a synthesizer to a banjo any day. The twang of a steel guitar and the crooning about lost love drive me up a tree. If my only choice was to go to a church where the music style was right out of Nashville, I probably would not go to church at all. Is it logical that a person would abandon the church over music? No, but people do not always make sense. They do what feels good. There are people walking the malls in every part of America for whom traditional church music has as little appeal as country music has for me. So, if our rule is: "To come to Christ, you must like organs and choirs," they won't come. Rick Warren asks, "When is the last time you heard an organ or choir on the radio?" It just is not listened to by most Americans. Does it make sense? Not really. And neither did it make sense for Paul to have Timothy circumcised *after* the knock-out victory at the Jerusalem Conference over this very issue. It made no sense unless throwing a rope to lost people is more important than just about anything except moral absolutes. And, as far as I can see, there is nothing morally absolute about organs and choirs. I do like organs and choirs, especially big ones, but they make little sense to Unchurched Harry and his friends.

Picture a biker: leather jacket and boots, hairy chest, beard, and a Harley Davidson parked outside while he sits in the third row of your church this Sunday. Is the service going to make sense to him? Is it going to relate to him on a cultural level? If you were a missionary from Brazil and had come to evangelize bikers in America, would you design such a service to reach him? No. The biker will not have a rational explanation for this; he just feels that Christianity must not be for people like him. It is for *other* people and that is fine, but it is not for him. Similarly, if *I* had ever had to do church "country style," I would not have done it at all. During my formative years, I would have opted out. Illogical, perhaps, but I would have said that Christianity must not be for people like me, who like contemporary/Top 40 sounds.

All of this illustrates only the drawing power of different music styles. There is much more to a ministry than music. The approach of the preaching, dress, the liturgy (or lack of it), the advertising media, and a host of other things must be considered in the marketing mix. "Different strokes for different folks"—but we cannot afford enough buildings to accommodate every group. On the other hand, the multi-congregational approach allows us to specialize, to focus on specific audiences at different times, without the overhead cost of hundreds of thousands of dollars every time we want to go after a new group. We can reach the unreached without turning off the already-committed.

George Barna is one of the most respected Christian trend-watchers of our day. His company, the Barna Research Group, has done consulting for Visa and the Disney Channel, as well as such Christian organizations as Focus on the Family and the Billy Graham Association. Bill Hybels says about him, "I try to read everything George Barna writes . . . not only because I *want* to—but because I feel I *have* to."[24] In a section of his book entitled *"Challenges and Opportunities for Churches; Vary the Menu,"* Barna writes, "For the church to consistently garner attendance and involvement at events and programs, there must be a great variety of what is offered."[25]

Next time you go to a fast-food eatery, try this little experiment. Look at each individual you pass and ask yourself, "What kind of ministry would I design to go after that person?" I hope you can see that it would be different for a sixty-five-year-old white man, an affluent Baby Boomer, a fourteen-year-old Hispanic youth, an Asian immigrant, a staid middle-aged couple from Oklahoma, a professor of music at the local university.

Think about these questions, too:

73

- Why do some churches feature high-church music?
- How can people stand to attend churches with yelling-and-screaming, hang-them-over-hell preachers?
- Why do people carry on so exuberantly at charismatic churches?
- How do super-legalistic churches attract people?
- Why isn't everyone normal—like me?

There are high-church churches, hang-them-over-hell churches, charismatic churches, legalistic churches, and countless others because it takes all kinds of churches to reach all kinds of people!

Peter Wagner points out that today's young people will not be reached by the churches of bygone days: "One of the immediate implications of rapid culture change is that the many members of the new generation will not be won to Christ in their parents' churches."[26] He adds, "Unbelievers come in such a wide variety that a correspondingly wide variety of church options is needed to win them."[27]

I recently heard a pastor talk about the demographics of the area he served. He had done his homework, recognizing that within a three-mile radius of his church was a wide range of socioeconomic and cultural backgrounds. He talked about how the local community really needed several (perhaps half a dozen) new congregations. Why weren't they started? They cost too much.

The multi-congregation model opens the door for ministry geared to specific groups of people. This is the kind of ministry Paul spoke of when he said:

> Though I am free and belong to no man, I make myself a slave to everyone, to win as many as possible. To the Jews I became like a Jew, to win the Jews. To those under the law I became like one under the law (though I myself am not under the law), so as to win those under the law. To those not having the law I became like one not having the law

(though I am not free from God's law but am under Christ's law), so as to win those not having the law. To the weak I became weak, to win the weak. I have become all things to all men so that by all possible means I might save some. [1 Cor. 9:19–22]

6. It capitalizes on the well-tested principle that new units grow faster than old units.

Peter Wagner writes, "The single most effective evangelistic methodology under heaven is planting new churches."[28] He notes that Lyle Schaller has said, "Every denomination reporting an increase in membership reports an increase in the number of congregations. Every denomination reporting an increase in the total number of congregations reports an increase in the members. Every denomination reporting a decrease in membership reports a decrease in congregations. Every denomination reporting a decrease in congregations reports a decrease in members."[29] Such information certainly suggests that starting more congregations would be pleasing to God. Yet, as we have seen, the major hurdle to starting new churches is the cost of constructing new facilities.

However, we can start a "new" church in *an existing building* with no capital expenditure. We can hire a mission pastor (or whatever way seems best to launch this) and begin capitalizing on the best evangelistic tool known to man— starting new churches. These new churches may be either a part of the larger family of the existing church or separate autonomous units. Those options are dealt with in a later chapter, but the principle holds true regardless of the details of organization.

7. There will be a synergy of congregations, with pastors and staffs working together toward a common goal.

Businesses that begin as partnerships consistently have a higher success rate than those started as sole proprietorships. People tend to get discouraged when working alone. That is why Jesus sent the disciples out two by two, and why the early church had teams of elders. As stated earlier, John R. W. Stott sees this as a major incongruence between the early church and the modern church.

Idea sharing and mutual encouragement can make each member of the team play better and thereby strengthen the total effort. If you have ever sung in a choir with someone who reads music well, you understand synergy. I can sing any part if sitting by the right person. (I know the meaning of the phrase, "I have grown taller from walking among trees.") George Barna says, "The most pervasive ministry frustration expressed by pastors is that they feel they bear the burden of ministry alone. Relatively few pastors feel they are part of a team of people working together to enhance the spiritual and social condition of the congregation and the world."[30]

The multi-congregation model allows laborers to work in a team environment. The synergy attained through mutual encouragement, idea sharing, and pooled knowledge is highly superior to the traditional Lone Ranger style of church planting.

8. There will be a more efficient use of equipment: videos, instruments, educational materials, and other tangible resources.

Not only will a church building be used more frequently, so will much of its other resources. Advertising can promote all the congregations that meet there. A common library, bookstore, and tape collection can benefit all the units. Names can be networked to pinpoint the most appropriate congregation for a particular person to attend. Hardware and software can be shared; a theological library can be a resource to every pastoral leader; one receptionist can service everyone. Besides the efficiency of this from a business viewpoint, God has promised that he will bless us in proportion to our faithfulness in managing worldly resources.

9. It capitalizes on the multi-service advantage.

Experts and objective evidence agree that there are big payoffs in having more than one worship service, even if overcrowding is not the reason for such an arrangement. We have seen it in our church. Each time we have added a service, total attendance has increased virtually overnight. Schaller calls this "the most effective means for increasing worship attendance."[31] This agrees with what experts have found nationwide. According to Rowland Crowder:

> Experimentation accompanied by diligent research on the part of church leaders has produced some revealing discoveries associated with the multiple use of church buildings. Some of these favorable findings are summarized here:
>
> * Multiple use reaches more people. Worship attendance and Sunday School attendance increased during multiple use of the buildings.
> * Finances increased in proportion to the numerical rise in attendance.
> * Buildings planned for multiple use schedule occupy less ground coverage.
> * Maintenance and custodial costs decreased in proportion to the number of persons in attendance.
> * Furnishing needs were reduced by approximately forty percent in ratio to attendance.
> * More time was allowed for better long-range building planning.
> * There was a substantial saving in utility costs in ratio to attendance.[32]

Although Crowder also mentioned some internal problems that need to be addressed, he added that most of them can be solved through administrative techniques. If dual services have advantages over one service, it follows that having ten or fifteen services a week under the ministry of several preaching pastors, musicians, and related staff will have further advantages over the two- or three-service system.

10. The multi-congregation model has the potential of being a big winner in terms of church growth.

Of course, there is no guarantee of success. The concept of growth requires an act of faith based on clear, biblical thinking. But because it has such far-reaching potential, I believe this is a venture worthy of experimentation. The potential gains are worth the risk. Willow Creek Community Church in Chicago decided to experiment with a multi-congregation model for that reason. Pastor Bill Hybels said at the time, "My vision, and it is totally supported by the elders, is that we will be the first mega-church to ever break the rule that unless the senior pastor teaches all the time, the church goes into the tank. If we can grow through this era, I say 'watch out.'"[33] Willow Creek now has four preaching pastors. Two years later, the world is still watching and the church is alive and still growing.

Let me be clear that when I say this idea is a real winner, I am not saying it is heaven. It is still hard work, and it requires skilled leadership to get the job done right. People who thrive best in the multi-congregational environment have a high tolerance for ambiguity. Those lacking that tolerance tend to get frustrated in such a church. Lyle Schaller wrote me to say, "Please do not promote this as a low cost or easy alternative! That is contrary to what I see experience demonstrates. It is a *very* high cost alternative . . . but if people are willing to pay the price, it is worth it."

John Maxwell, pastor of Skyline Wesleyan Church in San Diego, had a similar comment for me. In a phone conversation, he reminded me that good leaders can make a church grow, even with a bad system. Poor leaders, on the other hand, cannot bring about growth, even with a good system. He warned against looking at the multi-congregation paradigm as a surefire fix that can overcome poor leadership habits. "It is good leadership, not the model, that will keep the church growing," he told me. John went on to say that he felt the model was a good one and will be more and more needed in the days ahead. He had called to encourage me to get this message out.

Bear Valley Baptist Church in Denver is another example of a satisfied customer of the multi-congregation model. "We have developed multiple congregations and we have ten services each Sunday morning, one of them in a Jr. High School," says the former Senior Pastor. They have multiple *locations* as well as multiple times and offer a great variety of worship services.

Another example of a multi-congregation church is Perimeter Presbyterian in Atlanta. Pastor Randy Pope came to Atlanta in 1976 with a vision of impacting Atlanta for Christ, but not necessarily to build a mega-church. (There can be a difference between growing a church and expanding the kingdom.) There are now five campuses, each offering multiple services. Each campus has actually organized itself as a separate, autonomous unit that participates voluntarily in Perimeter Ministries, which functions in some ways as its own denomination. They are all, however, cooperating, *multi-congregational,* Presbyterian churches.

The following description of Ed Young's Second Baptist Church of Houston, the "Fellowship of Excitement," appeared in the *Wall Street Journal:*

> When it comes to worship, there is something for everyone. Currently, Mr. Young is in the midst of a Sunday morning sermon series entitled "How to Make Your Marriage Sizzle." As he cites biblical chapters and verses to drive home his points, some well-dressed listeners take notes.

For a hipper, mostly single crowd, there is "P. M. Houston," a Sunday evening service with guitar sing-alongs and lights that transform the sanctuary walls from aqua to rose. Wednesday nights, older folks gather for traditional hymns and preaching at the "Ripple Creek Gathering," while, in a separate chapel, teenagers sway and clap at "Solid Rock," a service in which a rock band sings Christian lyrics.[34]

This is the multi-congregation church in action. Notice four distinct worship formats, ranging from traditional to modern rock. Because each service targets a particular audience, the dress is different, the music is different, even the lights are different. There is no way that the needs of all four groups could be met in one service. And someone in Houston was smart enough to have figured that out.

Doug Murren needs to be included in the list of pastors excited about the multi-congregation approach. At one point his church had Friday-night services, Saturday-night services, and six services on Sunday. Initially they had these services just to contain the crowds, but later discovered the great advantage of offering these choices. Murren recommends that brand-new churches start with at least two services. This says to the community, "We are ready when you are."[35]

After he read my manuscript, I asked Dale Galloway about his church, New Hope Community Church in Portland, Oregon.

"Well," he said, "we have three services on Sunday."

"Anything on Monday?" I prompted.

"We have our New Life Victorious recovery groups on Monday night."

"And on Tuesday night?"

"The singles meet, and our singles minister does the preaching."

"What about Wednesday?"

"Most of our TLC—Tender Loving Care—groups meet on Wednesday."

"Do you have anything else going on?"

"On Thursday night the youth have Discipleship."

This sounds an awful lot like Acts 5:42: "Day after day, in the temple courts and from house to house, they never stopped teaching and proclaiming the good news that Jesus is the Christ." A curious thing about our conversation is that Dale, the senior pastor, was not absolutely sure how many services they do have—if you count recovery ministries, youth ministries, singles ministries, and so on. That kind of church qualifies as multi-congregational.

In a tape on Transformative Leadership, Frank Tillapaugh gives a more extreme example: The Wesleyan Mission in Sydney has forty-five congregations! Yet the leadership noticed they were still missing a slice of the urban pie. They were reaching the Chinese population, but only those who drove a Mercedes. Were there no poor Chinese in the area? Yes, there were, but where were they? Who were they? Mainly illegal aliens who worked in the restaurants as busboys and dishwashers. So the mission sent its staff down the alleyways and back streets to ask these people when they could come to church. Not on Sundays, since they were busy earning a bare livelihood by serving the people who go out to eat after church on Sundays. The mission discovered the optimum worship time for these poor, working-class Chinese to be from midnight to 2:00 A.M.—after they got off work. This was convenient for the mission, too, for even with forty-five congregations the building had not been used during this time.

Jamie Buckingham agrees with this concept. Speaking of churches that are really effective today, he says, "They know it's fruitless to invest in big auditoriums and small nurseries. Instead, they build huge children's facilities and hold multiple services in their smaller auditoriums."[36]

Churches like these are realizing that the multi-congregational approach has staggering growth potential. Only 20 percent of the churches in America are growing. When they do grow, sooner or later they run out of space. So they build. This will normally kill their growth, according to Chaney and Lewis, who write: "Do not be surprised if decline or no growth for a year or two follows the construction and occupation of a new building. This is most often what really happens."[37] We are not sure why, but there are so few examples of American churches that have consistently grown through more than two major building programs that it is statistically negligible. The multi-congregation church has the chance to break out of this impasse. Using this idea will not cause a plateaued or declining church to grow, but it can remove one obstacle that keeps growing churches from *continuing* to grow.

If the multi-congregational approach was only a minor improvement, we could choose to ignore it. If we were not in desperate need of help, we could continue with business as usual. So we have to ask ourselves if the problems are bad enough to warrant this kind of fundamental change. The answer must be "Yes!" if we are serious about the Great Commission.

The problems facing us are enormous. Church growth in an entire country, one of the leading Christian nations of the world, is at a standstill. Southern Baptists, though 38,000 churches strong, have been corporately on plateau for a generation. Many other denominations have actually declined in membership. If I read the Great Commission correctly, this is in direct violation of the command of God. The church must be a living body with measurable growth. This is not happening! I cannot help but think that God is concerned about this and might even be very angry with us.

This is no small matter, but going back to the pattern of the early church seems to be a large part of the answer. I have lived with this idea for some time now, and its potential has come to grip me in a profound way. Although there are costs and trade-offs in terms of time and trouble, I have become convinced more and more each day that God is calling this generation to do something special, something really significant toward advancing his kingdom. This generation is facing demographic conditions that have never before existed. Never has the world seen this kind of size and diversity of population. Half the people that have ever lived since Adam are alive today (roughly 10 billion have been born on this planet, and 5 billion are living now). The population explosion and urbanization have driven the costs of new facilities out of sight, but every time we use our existing buildings, we release more of the $85 billion[38] in kingdom assets to kingdom work. If we can give to the next generation a church that is growing and has the potential to continue to grow, we will have served our Lord as faithful stewards. We must vigorously explore the possibilities of the multi-congregation church, which I firmly believe is the most practical way to further that objective.

5

Questions About the
Multi-Congregation Church

If the multi-congregation church is a biblically allowable concept, and if it is demonstrated that it has practical advantages over the traditional and multi-service model, it stands to reason that Christians everywhere will readily adopt the idea. Right?

Wrong!

Sincere Christians may still have several questions. I will attempt to answer ten of them in this chapter.

Question 1
Wouldn't a multi-congregation approach increase staff burnout?

I am totally opposed to any plan that advances the work at the expense of the worker. We simply cannot afford to overload our ministerial staff and lay workers to the point of burnout! If the roots of a tree are undernourished, that tree will eventually wither and die, starting with its trunk. When the tree cracks and falls, new leaves may continue to sprout on its branches, but they, too, will eventually die. The leaders of a church—whether staff or laypeople—are its support system. If they fall, they crush the life spirits of all those to whom they minister.

I am not suggesting a plan that will put church leaders on a collision course with breakdown. In a multi-congregation church, each of the staff can come to the church the same number of times as in the traditional model. (It may take a little time for the staff to get used to not being present for every church activity.) I recommend that leaders work a normal work week, take days off, and spend time with their families. Some staff members could even do their work for services during the week and take a real weekend when their kids are out of school. The staff's time would have to be monitored to prevent burnout, but that is even necessary with the traditional model. If we answered every request on our time, if we pursued every good idea, if we did everything that every member thought would be good for the church, we staff members would soon be exhausted. This is true of most people, regardless of vocation. We all must learn to say "no" to some things. It is not a busy schedule that burns out a person, unless it becomes an outlet for workaholism. The real problem for kingdom workers is the drivenness that must be tamed, ultimately, by the power of the gospel.

Multiple services are not the only possible cause of burnout and stress for the pastor and staff. Debt has a way of adding even greater pressure. Exhibit A: Norm Boshoff, pastor of the fast-growing Hoffmantown Baptist Church in Albuquerque. It was not when the church was holding four services that he burned out. It was when he felt the weight of a $6-million debt. I heard a man who had been a member of that church for many years say, "I have never seen a building program that did not destroy a pastor."

"How many building programs have you been in?" I queried.

"Six" (not all at Hoffmantown). Multiple services are not the only thing that can burn out the pastor or staff.

Consider the following excerpt from *Leadership* magazine:

> WOOD: When the church [Central Christian] committed to this and plans were drawn in 1975, cost estimates were $2.2 million. But, with inflation, increasing costs, and changes in design, things grew and grew, and before we knew it, we had a $6.4 million dollar project. In 1980 the church moved [to its new location]. I resigned in mid 1981.
>
> LEADERSHIP: What went wrong?
>
> WOOD: Total concentration was forced into the financial area. We were determined this would not happen, but no matter how we tried, everything came back to raising the budget every week—pushing, pushing, pushing.[1]

One consideration in adopting a multi-congregation plan will be to keep consistent the ratio of staff to attendance. It would be easy to think that if a pastor can preach to three hundred people, he can turn around and do it again to another three hundred. And he can, as long as we understand that we must provide for the other needs of these people through additional programs and staff.

Question 2
Isn't it wrong to violate church tradition by changing long-accepted practices?

"We have met the enemy and it is us," someone once said. Our own tradition-bound mind-set will no doubt be our biggest obstacle. Elmer Towns calls this fear of new things the disease of innovitis.[2] It is one of the most deadly diseases known to churches. Peter Wagner says the greatest barriers to church planting are in the mind.[3] The same could be said for adopting the multi-congregational model.

Traditions are nothing to take lightly. Consider Peter when confronted by a vision of an angel telling him to eat food forbidden by Jewish law. God himself, through the person of the angel, is telling him to eat, yet Peter responds, "Surely not, Lord" (Acts 10:14). Consider the irony of those two words. Tradition is a strong force, a collection of habits that are hard to break or revise. On the other hand, tradition can be a very good thing and should not be lightly discarded.

We stand on the shoulders of giants. If it were not for the faith of those who went before us, our own hopes and sense of purpose would not exist. We have enjoyed and profited by the institutions they built and used the organizations they set in place. We have been inspired by their heroism, which brought them at times even to dying for the convictions they held. They have taught us much in every way. Of many of them it could be said, as it was of David, "He served God in his generation and he died." I have high praise for the saints who have gone before us. May future generations find us just as faithful.

In the parable of the wineskins (Matt. 9:17), Jesus taught that it is our responsibility to present the gospel and organize its fruit in new ways that are appropriate to our generation. This does not mean following the way of the world, nor is it disloyal to our spiritual forefathers. It is a call to be "as shrewd as snakes and as innocent as doves" (Matt. 10:16). We are not to tamper with the content—the wine—but unless the wine is placed in new wineskins, it will be lost. The hard reality is that the rich wine of the gospel is being wasted in America. It has not been given enough room to expand. Could the wineskin be the problem? Perhaps not overseas, but we have not seen the American church advance significantly in fifty years. Jesus' teaching on the nature of the church tells us that there is something wrong. The church is a living entity that must be allowed to grow. Non-growth for the church is an aberration.

Jesus handed us the keys to the kingdom and promised that all the defenses of hell could not stop the advancement of his kingdom if we properly used the power he gave to us. We are stewards of God's most precious treasure—the means by which his children can enter heaven.

Although we cannot know for certain how effectively the multi-congregation model would remedy the church's current stagnation, I believe we are bound by the commands of Jesus to try to pull ourselves out of our non-growth mode by whatever means are possible. A method that would result in placing many more laborers in the harvest field certainly has the potential of increasing our ability to fulfill the Great Commission, and it is solidly based on the teaching of Jesus. He even pointed out that tradition can be the enemy of the church, saying scornfully to the Pharisees, "You have let go of the commands of God and are holding on to the traditions of men" (Mark 7:8).

As changes go, this may be an easy one to implement. You will not be *forcing* people to change their worship schedule. All those who want to continue attending as usual may do so. All they are being asked to do is to *grant permission* for new groups and/or new congregations to meet at alternate times. There *will* be some subtle overall changes. For example, as staff responsibilities are shared, everyone will be affected. People who used to attend a particular service may choose to attend at a different time, thus losing some contact with friends who do not make the change. But because the changes will be minimal, the rights of those who want to enjoy church as they always have will be protected. We must be committed to meeting the needs of everyone.

Many long-time members have given their lives for the church. They deserve to feel comfortable and welcome there. Yet, there is another generation to reach. Those born after World War II are far less likely to attend church than their parents. Reaching this generation and their children will require a different approach. The multi-congregational approach gives us the opportunity to meet the needs of older church members and, at the same time, offer services that will appeal to Americans under forty, many of whom have been unchurched.

George Barna points out that the real rewards go to those who are innovative and daring: "The denominations that will make the greatest headway in the '90s will not be the mainline churches, but those which are smaller and are willing to take greater risks."[4] The real issue is: Will we give to our children a tradition of a church that is obedient to the Great Commission? I realized how quickly tradition can change from one generation to the next when I had to explain to my son that most people go to church on Sunday morning. Since he was two, Dawson has known only Saturday night church. "Why would anyone want to go to church on Sundays?" was his reply. I believe I am giving him a better tradition.

Question 3
If I like going to church on Sundays because it is convenient, why should I change?

It is worthwhile to discuss whether or not the multi-congregation church is biblical and how it might help us fulfill the Great Commission. However, to argue that it would simply be "inconvenient" for individuals to worship at a different time than they are accustomed to is to portray a carnal selfishness that I trust is not present in the church. It was not convenient for Jesus to leave heaven. Neither is it convenient for missionaries to leave their families and friends, and give up all the amenities of life at home, and raise their kids in a foreign culture. When a traditional church moves to the multi-congregation model, the pastor will do more preaching, at least initially. This, too, may not be convenient. But should we let convenience be our guiding value in deciding how best to implement God's kingdom?

In addition, let me point out that no one's lifestyle will have to be modified unless he or she voluntarily chooses to do so. What will likely happen is that a church will continue to have one or more services on Sundays and *add* more services, both on Sunday and during the week. The latter will be populated primarily by people who do not have a strong Sunday-worship tradition. When I used to teach a class for young married adults on Saturday nights, I noticed that out of about thirty-five people, only three couples had previously attended Sunday-morning services. The rest had joined the church *after* we started the Saturday sessions. What this showed me is that we need to grant permission for people who are not now going to church to come at a nontraditional time. The point is not to get people who go on Sunday to change to some other day. Instead, we must provide space and opportunity for those who have not been attending at all.

Even the most multi-congregational of churches will always have at least one worship service on Sunday. In fact, for many years to come, most worship services will probably be on Sunday. But there will also be many other worship services. The issue is not so much related to days of the week as it is to the specific needs of each congregational unit served by a particular church.

A church may need to make appeals for people to move from an existing service to newly created alternatives, whether on weeknights or at an additional time on Sunday. Some of the people who change times may migrate back after the new service gets established. When churches start or sponsor daughter churches, they often ask their members to attend the new unit for a while to help get it on firm ground. The multi-congregational pattern is similar. What we are doing is providing choices, not mandating attendance at certain times.

Question 4

Some people will give to buildings but not to anything else. Would the multi-congregational approach cut off a church from certain resources?

We all have several pockets and practice selective giving. Some like to give to the general budget; some like to give to education, or to missions, or to special projects. And some will only give to buildings. Although the physical plant is important, even with the multi-congregational approach, here the emphasis shifts from what *new* buildings might be needed immediately to how best to utilize (and improve) existing facilities. A multi-congregation church will draw even more resources if it can communicate to people that it is talking about a building that will be used maybe ten or fifteen times a week. In the minds of building-fixated members, the only down side is that the multi-congregation church can continue to add services and thus lessen the need for bigger and grander buildings.

Actually, a multi-congregation church needs a well-planned building far more than a traditional church, which can survive temporarily in a school or other rented facility. This just would not be practical for a multi-congregation church. It needs a building that can be used every day for a multiplicity of services and ministries.

The truth is, building campaigns tend to be hard on churches, as has already been pointed out. There are so many battles to fight and decisions to make that the pastor may be wounded by the crossfire. Chaney and Lewis, authors of *Design for Church Growth,* discuss "architectural evangelism," a term Schaller has described as the belief that "we are going to build this building and people will be drawn to it like a magnet." Chaney and Lewis point out that despite such optimism, the opposite is usually true. Attendance will normally decline after a construction program. In a conversation with Charles Chaney, he said that this observation was based on an actual study of churches in Illinois before and after a building project. His explanation for this drop was primarily the diversion of attention from evangelism and church growth to construction and fund-raising details.

A recent *Newsweek* poll indicated that people are more worried about money today than they have been in years.[5] In answer to the question, "Are you generally satisfied with your standard of living, with what it can do or buy?" only 62 percent of the sample answered in the affirmative, as compared to 82 percent of those surveyed ten years ago. Answers to more specific questions revealed that people were not so much concerned with affording things not yet affordable, as they were worried about hanging on to what they already had. That is why, when churches constantly ask for more money, they do not always find their members as responsive as they had hoped. This is not necessarily a spiritual problem; it is a financial one, with national implications.

Question 5
How will we maintain the unity of the church and keep from becoming splintered? How will I get to know people who attend alternate services?

Two separate issues are on the table here. One is the issue of multiple congregations; the other involves the size of the total church body. One of the things that usually happens as a church becomes larger is that people become uncomfortable with all these "strangers" around them every week. This is true of *any* growing church, whether traditional or multi-congregational.

In fact, the multi-congregation church has the advantage of diminishing this problem. In the traditional large-church approach, we place people in a huge auditorium where it is difficult to get to know people. In the multi-congregational approach, the same people may be spread out across ten services. For an individual, it will feel more like he or she is attending a small church. People come in, sit down in a modest auditorium, and see familiar faces. No matter that there are hundreds of other anonymous people who attend at alternate times. We have had people join our church because they like the feel of a smaller church when in fact we are larger than the church they come from.

There is a deeper, spiritual issue here. We must be willing for more people to come to Christ than we can know personally. After all, how many names can you learn? I hit my limit during the summer of 1989. The hard disk is full. Every time I learn a new one, I have to forget an old one. (And I can't be as selective as I would like as to whom to forget!) But I still want more and more people to come to faith. Although some of our members have said to us flat out, "We are growing too fast," their frustration was that they could not get to know *everyone*.

Darla, one of our secretaries, helped me with this point by saying, "These people who think the church is growing too fast need to come in and tell me which names I should strike from the membership roll. To whom should we deny membership?"

Research has demonstrated that in the small church the average person knows about sixty-five people. In the large church also, the average person knows about that same number. In other words, the size of the church has nothing to do with how many people one knows. The real issue is allowing the gospel to spread wider than any particular circle of "friends."

Question 6
If it ain't broke, don't fix it.

Some would argue that the multi-congregational approach may indeed have some advantages, but why bother? The church has gotten along fine without it for many years, so why try to fix something that is not broken? And I agree: If the plane is flying level, don't fiddle with the knobs.

But I argue that the church is in a serious state of affairs. A whole generation is largely unreached by the message of the gospel. For as long as I have been alive, the church has been at a standstill. A church in the leading Christian nation of the world (at least for now) is corporately ineffective in carrying out the task our Lord gave us to do. There has been no growth in the percentage of adults who are born-again Christians.[6] Barna writes, "Most Christians do not perceive the church to be in the midst of the most severe struggle it has faced in centuries."[7] The proportion of people who become formal members of a church will eventually decline to less than 50 percent of the adult population. Adherence to a Protestant church will drop from the current 45 percent to about 38 percent. Church attendance on Sunday mornings will decrease to about 35 percent of the population on any given weekend. Barna adds, "This figure would drop lower if it were not for the growing number of congregations that will change the long-standing pattern and offer worship services on Saturdays, and on Sunday afternoons, in addition (or, occasionally instead of) the traditional Sunday morning time."[8]

In *The Problem of WineSkins,* Howard Snyder begins his book with a sweeping statement about the lack of effectiveness of the church in this generation. Although I think Snyder may have overstated the case, the fact that he can say it and still receive such widespread acceptance is significant: "It is hard to escape the conclusion that today one of the greatest roadblocks to the gospel of Jesus Christ is the institutional church."[9] No, it is probably not that bad—at least, I hope it is not.

Ralph Neighbor has been watching churches for thirty-five years. His evaluation cuts to the quick: "In light of this population explosion in the world, we must conclude that current models of church planting are inadequate."[10] And again, "A more realistic evaluation may simply be that the old ways of 'doing church' in the 1990's neither satisfies those who are inside nor outside the structures."[11] Please, tell me he is wrong—tell me everything is okay. Tell me that God has not noticed our lack of effectiveness in terms of the Great Commission.

Perhaps it is time we heeded the advice of Gene Getz: "It is time for the church to evaluate the kinds of meetings it has, and to justify their existence on the basis of New Testament principles and purposes."[12]

If it ain't broke. . . . But it is! Let's face the facts. If a car does not drive, we say it is broken. If a pen does not write, we say it is broken. If a church fails to fulfill its God-given purpose, we must say it is broken. The first step toward recovery for an alcoholic is the admission that he or she has a problem. I have gone to denominational meetings where the speakers say, "We had a good year in our churches this year—attendance was down, conversions were down, membership was down—but we had some good meetings." That's a cop-out!

The multi-congregation church cannot provide all the answers. A church will need to get some other things right to survive in the next century. It will need to pray right, to preach right, to do small-group ministry right. But it can do all these things right and still be "broken," in terms of its mission, if it is spending $6,000 per person on buildings.

Question 7

How is the multi-congregation church best organized?

Although several possibilities would be open in considering the organization of the multi-congregation church, a decade of experimentation in a variety of places and denominations will be necessary before we get a handle on what the *best* options are. For example, each "congregation" could be an independent, autonomous local church that met on one night of the week and/or a specific time on Saturday and Sunday. In this model the parent body would simply launch the congregation and then cut ties with its members, except for being paid rent for use of the facilities. They could eventually choose to move to different rented quarters or construct their own building. However, I do not think this method is the best.

We once sponsored a multi-congregation church-planting venture that accommodated two separate, autonomous churches—one Spanish and one English—in the same building. But this was a little like forcing two cats to live together by knotting their tails together. If they fussed, it was no use reminding them that they were Christians who shouldn't behave like that. In such an arrangement, no one really has the pride of ownership of the building. There is no inherent unity and few opportunities for face-to-face interaction between the congregations. Nevertheless, the First Korean Baptist Church of Silver Springs, Maryland, has made this idea work. It sponsored autonomous churches in a building it owned, and the satellite groups were in a renters' posture. (In our case, although both groups owned the building, each tended to resent the other being there.)

Another possibility would be to have multiple congregations within *one* church body. Under the direction of the senior pastor, a designated staff member would work with one (or two) of the weekday congregations. Instead of having a "minister for youth," you would have a "minister for

97

Monday night." This has the advantage of identifying the lines of responsibility. The Monday-night pastor would be responsible for *everything* to do with Monday night. The sense of ownership of that corner of the ministry would motivate him (or her) to see that Monday services succeeded. Another advantage to this plan is the familiar pastor-to-people relationship that will be maintained. For people who don't like a "preacher of the week" plan, this retains the value of knowing who will be in the pulpit every Monday. It has the feel of the traditional church, even though worship is at a nontraditional time.

On the other hand, there are educational advantages in listening to more than one preacher (as mentioned earlier). When a church gets to the point that it is attracting people who are only willing to hear the truth from one mouthpiece, it is not creating disciples but pastor worshipers. This is not a religious experience; it is a show. It is not true Christianity; it is idolatry. If a church has only one preaching pastor available, that is one thing; if parishioners *refuse* to listen to the gospel from more than one person, that is another.

This model does hold a strategic advantage in the launching of new congregations. We have learned two things about starting new congregations—people move in groups, and people follow leaders (more on this later). If the pastor of the 9:45 Sunday service says he is starting a Monday-night service and will no longer be preaching at the usual time, he is almost certain to get a group to move out of personal loyalty to him. They will go in a group and they will follow his leadership.

A still-unanswered question related to this arrangement is whether it would be best for the senior pastor to serve just one of the congregations, or to apportion his leadership among all the groups, preaching at each of the services from time to time (or even not at all). This would give him an objectivity that none of the other preaching pastors would have. If a senior pastor has a home turf of only one congregation, it might be difficult for him to be evenhanded in the allocation of resources within the overall body, whereas real or perceived favoritism might be alleviated if the leader has no particular loyalty to one group.

Another model has several preaching pastors who are corporately responsible for overseeing the whole church (with one as a senior pastor). They would work out a preaching schedule so that all of them would be periodically heard by each congregation. This is the preaching-team concept employed at Willow Creek. It has the advantage of allowing people to learn from the gifts of several teaching pastors. Other staff would work with various groups and specialized ministries as the need existed. One of the things we have learned from doing the Saturday-night service and the 9:45 Sunday service is that people tend to worship in homogeneous groups. For example, there are very few youth who attend either of these congregations. I suspect this will always be true. It would be unusual for a church to have several congregations that were demographically similar, nor would it be particularly desirable. This diversity would have an impact on the way staff worked. A church may not need a youth minister to service a congregation composed primarily of senior adults. Visitors could be networked and steered toward the congregation and the pastor that most appropriately meet their needs. Although this is my preferred model, all of those mentioned retain some of the advantages of the multi-congregational approach.

I don't think we can discover the best way to organize a multi-congregation church with a sharp pencil alone. Experimentation will teach us far more than head scratching, even when done by very smart people. The best thinking on the multi-congregation church has not yet been done. I need you to do some of it. Every multi-congregation church need not organize itself the same way. We need to be released from the weight of a system wherein lack of flexibility forestalls the rapid expansion of the body of Christ. There may be several good ways to create disciples and encourage church growth.

Question 8
How much building is too much?

A good rule-of-thumb about physical facilities is what I call the Law of 15. No more than 15 percent of the budget should go to new construction, except in very rare circumstances. Going above this percentage can have negative results. The good news is that most churches can do 15 percent every year without hurting the growth of the church. Some people like to give toward bricks, lumber, and nails!

The Law of 15 also means that a church should invest no more than $1,500 per person in capital items. If you have 1,000 attending, your total facilities should value no more than $1.5 million. If you are transitioning from a traditional model, as we are, this may take years to accomplish, but it is attainable in the multi-congregation model. And all the rest goes to ministry.

Question 9
How can we keep the multi-church from getting out of control?

"Decently, and in order," is the rally cry of those who need a sense that all is progressing under the supervision of a competent leader, a well-written plan, and a well-managed staff. Honesty dictates an admission that the multi-congregation organization is more difficult to control than a traditional church—just as an association of churches (or district, presbytery, or diocese) is more difficult to control than a single unit. But that is no reason to be against the idea, if it will further God's purposes. The point is this: Keeping things in control may not be the best objective. The wildfires of revival are inherently difficult to control.

Roland Allen has some insightful things to say about control and the work of God: "We fear that it [the spontaneous expansion of the church] is something that we cannot control. And it is true. We can neither induce nor control spontaneous expansion whether we look on it as the work of the individual or of the church. . . .'The wind blows where it will,' said Christ."[13]

So how are we to adjust to this lack of control? Allen helps us again:

> If we cannot control it, we ought to rejoice that we cannot control it. For if we cannot control it, it is because it is too great, not because it is too small for us. Therein lies the vast hope. Spontaneous expansion could fill the continents with the knowledge of Christ: our control cannot reach as far as that. We constantly bewail our limitations: open doors unentered; doors closed to us as foreign missionaries; fields white to the harvest which we cannot reap. Spontaneous expansion could enter open doors, force closed ones, and reap those white fields. Our control cannot: it can only appeal pitifully for more men to maintain control.[14]

Question 10
Will people feel comfortable attending church other than on Sunday?

There is a strong tradition for Sunday worship in America. This is true outside the church as well as within. Even people without a church background recognize Sunday as the day of worship. Sunday is a convenient time to attend church. The schools are not open, and many businesses are closed. It occupies a religious slot in people's minds. Why fight it?

This is a good question and deserves a thoughtful answer. It is also worthy of consideration that on several occasions the church, the *whole* church, has been dead wrong about its thinking and practice. For example, there was a time when it was the unquestioned understanding that the Scriptures should not be made available to untrained laymen. It was also once believed that salvation was obtained by grace through the sacraments of the church, and that church tradition was on equal footing with the Bible itself in terms of authority. Then came the Reformation.

There was a time, too, when the whole church felt that missionaries were unnecessary and were certainly more trouble than they were worth. Some Christian leaders not only ignored the cause of missions, they opposed it. Then came William Carey and the world-missions movement.

In each of these cases, the total thinking of the church, the paradigm in which the church operated, was eventually changed for the better. It could well be that God has raised us up for such a time as this.

John R. W. Stott is helpful on this point:

> Change is painful to all of us, especially when it affects our cherished buildings and customs, and we should not seek change merely for the sake of change. Yet, true Christian radicalism is open to change. It knows that God has bound himself to his church (promising that he will never leave it) and to his Word (promising that it will never pass away). But God's church means people not buildings, and God's Word means Scripture not tradition. So long as the essentials are preserved, the buildings and the traditions can go if necessary. We must not allow them to imprison the Living God or to impede his mission in the world.[15]

Part Two

Implementing the Multi-Congregation Model

6

Principles on Change from the Book of Acts

No matter how sincere, well-meaning, and intelligent a person may be, it is natural to resist and even fear any change in a long-established routine. Christians are not immune to this very human quality, so adjusting to the multi-congregational form of worship requires a leap of faith. Pastoral leaders tend to assume that once people understand the logic of a proposal for the church, everyone will hop on board like children on a carnival ride. This explains why we are in trouble all of the time!

I used to believe this would get easier over time. For example, I once thought of our young Saturday-night crowd as innovative, open to change, ready to try new ideas. *Wrong.* When we started the 12:15 Sunday service and I appealed to some of them to come along and help us launch the venture, I was rudely jolted back into reality.

"What? Attend on Sundays? Who in their right mind would want to attend church on Sundays?" How we love our traditions—even our new ones.

Lyle Schaller will sober us in his insight on change: "Anyone seriously interested in planned social change would be well advised to recognize two facts of life. First, despite the claims of many, relatively little is known about change. Second, much of what is known will not work."[1] He says later in his book *The Change Agent,* "The initial reaction of most people to a proposal to change will be negative."[2] It has always been that way.

I previously cited the example of Peter as a sincere, well-meaning, intelligent, and godly person who was resistant, very resistant, to change. It may be that there are people in your church like Peter. What you want to do for "Peter" is add new traditions to his spiritual repertoire—like launching a new service every year at Easter. When change is expected and prepared for, it more easily becomes part of the culture, a reality that we can live with and celebrate. Another example of how "tradition" can work *for* you is in the area of adding staff. Dissension within the congregation(s) about augmenting the church staff can be minimized if you establish the tradition of adding staff on a regular basis.

Whatever you do, try to change as little as possible. Set a new direction, get on course, and stay on course. Slow and steady wins the race, but a church that has established the tradition of adding services and adding staff combines the power of tradition with the vitality of change. Like the seasons, change can be refreshing, if it is anticipated.

I am indebted to Lyle Schaller for the terminology of the pioneers and the homesteaders, already mentioned in the first chapter. The pioneers came first and laid their claim to the territory. They have created certain traditions and will be predictably resistant to changing them. This does not mean they are bad people. It means they are normal. There will be just enough pioneers who are open to change to make you think that everyone else is open to change. Not so. Schaller again: "The change agent will have fewer frustrations and more successes if he assumes that in the face of change people will behave like normal human beings."[3]

Sometimes lovers of change are too open to the kind of change that could disrupt the fellowship. Those who resist change and love old-time tradition tend to give a church stability and resilience. They would be the first to fight a hostile takeover by an alien group. They know the church needs to keep on course and not sacrifice its basic objectives. This is all very well until there really *does* need to be a change. And in times like ours, change is not only inevitable, it is a necessary ingredient of our survival strategy.

Brand loyalty is virtually nonexistent in the post-World War II generation. In the spiritual realm, this translates to a large number of unaffiliated church shoppers. People do not come to church because they "ought to." Even less likely would they stay within a denomination simply because they grew up in that denomination. They will change churches, switch denominations, or just drop out of religious life *if their needs are not being met.* I am not saying this is good. I am saying it is true. Unless the church at large figures out a way to be flexible enough to adapt to a changing culture, it will not survive.

How do we smoothly make the transition from a traditional, established church to a multi-service church and then to a multi-congregational body with interlocking parts? (Even if the church stops at the multi-service point, it will be twice as effective as it was in the traditional model.) The good news is that the New Testament contains some wonderful guidelines for change management. It is called the Book of Acts, a narrative that is principally a history of the early church. From this evidence, we conclude that the Christian church began as a single, isolated cell in Jerusalem, a small group of about 120 believers who were meeting in fellowship and prayer soon after Christ's crucifixion, resurrection, and ascension, probably under the general leadership of Peter and some of the other apostles (see Acts 1:12–26). Luke's account spans about thirty years, and—by the end of that period—the body of Christ had become a burgeoning multi-national movement that was turning the world upside down. It was apparently made up of large city-wide, multi-congregation churches, or perhaps we could say "clusters" of churches. It was already a radically changed church, one that started out as a Jewish movement and pushed through to the Gentiles, even reaching the hated Samaritan culture and distant pagans.

The early church was often riddled with conflict, much of it based on doctrinal disagreements between the two major factions: the Jewish traditionalists and the Gentile converts. (Here we can see a parallel with the pioneer/home-steader analogy proposed by Schaller.) Nevertheless, the church continued to expand, which suggests that the Book of Acts contains some principles for effecting change, for overcoming the very normal reluctance to make some revisions in the traditions of the past. The story of the early church will serve as our guide.

Principle 1
Get some initial success.

People will not follow a "change agent" who merely speaks in rather vague terms about potential success or future growth. If there is no evidence in current reality, they will operate on the assumption that past experience is the only predictor we have of the future. Current growth *can* be projected into the future, but it is normal to assume that Mr. Murphy will enforce his law soon enough. It is very difficult for people to follow a leader if they see no signs of progress. Success breeds success. Most people will only follow a proven winner or a plan that seems to be working.

Imagine the leaders of the early church, trying to persuade their Jewish members to follow them in organizing a large multi-congregational, multi-national church that would include many Gentiles, whose cultural tradition was so different from their own. Suppose that after five years of ministry in Jerusalem, the church had grown from 120 to only 165. Some had come in and some had gone. So the disciples recall the life and teachings of Jesus and are reminded of the Great Commission. They discuss this and tell their fellow believers that they need to develop a missions program to the Gentiles. What are their chances of pulling off this change? Pretty slim.

Contrast this with what actually happened. Early success fueled their ability to effect change, which brought them even more success. As Schaller says, "To succeed in achieving the initial goal a person must aspire to attain it, but he is *unlikely to aspire unless he can see that the success is possible.*"[4]

Another example of this principle is Paul's success in reaching the Gentiles. God was saving them, so who could argue with Paul's missionary efforts? If Paul had tried to discuss the point before he had any converts, he would have had a much more difficult time. The early victories under his belt empowered him to earn further victories in terms of effecting change within the church body.

Leaders tend to blame others for lack of growth in the church. Pastors blame deacons or the board or "those old codgers." A more productive attitude for leaders to take is that they themselves are accountable. A leader must accept the responsibility to make things happen through the power of the Holy Spirit. After the leader is able to make something happen, people are more likely to follow.

Of course, the apostles did not cause Pentecost, nor directly work the miracles that followed, nor activate the explosive growth without God's empowering. But they showed themselves to be in the stream of what God was doing. This is what gives Christian leaders their legitimacy. God's blessing follows them and underwrites their successes.

Sam Shaw, our pastor, demonstrated this principle in a dramatic way. Just a few months after he arrived, he scheduled a "Nehemiah Sunday." This was to be a special fundraising occasion, with three tiers of goals, the highest being $40,000. On that one day, the church raised in excess of $60,000 to pay off some old debts! When the total was announced, the place was electric with joy. This early victory proved that Sam was in the stream of God's blessing, which set the stage for future victories by giving credibility to the changes he envisioned.

If you aspire to change your church into an aggressive, innovative, effective vehicle for God's blessing in fulfilling the Great Commission, the first focus must be inward. Discover what God is doing and what works. Then get in the flow and grab onto some early victories.

Principle 2
Develop some rock-solid convictions.

Let God help you decide what you will and will not change. Leadership starts in the closet. It starts in prayer. It starts on your knees. It starts with God-given convictions so profound that nothing will shake them. The hard reality is that some leaders must be martyrs for the greater good of the advancement of the kingdom. They may not die for their faith, but it may cost them dearly in other ways. Stephen was right as right can be, yet he was killed after his first sermon. Although onlookers might have thought that Stephen was a loser, the view was different from heaven. (See Acts 7.)

I pray we will give to the next generation a body of Christ that is positioned for much greater effectiveness than is the current church. It is *my* rock-solid conviction that the multi-congregation approach is a part of that. But

I am aware that some who share my belief may have to fall on their swords in their efforts to make this dream a reality.

Obviously, every church is not going to change, because conviction that a change is necessary is not enough to accomplish a change. Individuals willing to do what is necessary to implement change, to pay what may be a high price for their belief (or conviction), are a vital part of creating a new "tradition." Often we say, "I tried that, but it did not work." The truth is, we didn't try it long enough. Edison believed he could invent a light bulb. He tried three hundred different elements as the filament before he got one that worked. He could have said, "I tried making a light bulb, but I failed." Because he kept trying, we have electric lighting today.

Let me be perfectly frank with you (my middle name is Frank). Changing the traditional church to a multi-congregation model will not be easy. The idea will not be instantly and unanimously accepted. A few people are first going to have to develop some rock-solid convictions about the importance of accomplishing this change. They are going to have to want it strongly enough to suffer the slings and arrows of skeptics and nay-sayers.

Bennis and Nanus did a fascinating study of ninety leaders of American companies and organizations, whom they described as "right brained and left brained, tall and short, fat and thin, articulate and inarticulate, assertive and retiring, dressed for success and dressed for failure."[5] What did these executives have in common? "All ninety people interviewed had an *agenda,* an unparalleled concern with outcome. Leaders are the most results-oriented individuals in the world, and results get attention."[6] The authors quote this poem from Don Marquis, which is worth the price of the book:

The Lesson of the Moth

I was talking to a moth the other evening.
He was trying to break into an electric bulb and fry himself
  on the wire.
"Why do you fellows pull this stunt?" I asked him.
"Because it is a conventional thing for moths?
Or why, if that had been an uncovered candle, instead of an
  electric light bulb,
You would now be a small, unsightly cinder.
Have you no sense?"
"Plenty of it," he answered, "but at times we get tired of
  using it.
We get bored with the routine and crave beauty and excite-
  ment.
Fire is beautiful and we know that if we get too close it will
  kill us.
But what does it matter?
It is better to be happy for a moment and be burned up with
  beauty
Than to live a long time and be bored all the while.
So we roll all our life up into one little roll,
And then we shoot the roll.
That's what life is for.
It is better to be a part of beauty for one instant
And then cease to exist,
Than to exist forever and never be a part of beauty.
Our attitude toward life is
Come easy, go easy.
We're like human beings used to be before they became too
  civilized to enjoy themselves."
And before I could argue him out of his philosophy,
He went and immolated himself on a patented cigar lighter.
I do not agree with him.
Myself, I would rather have half the happiness
And twice the longevity.
But at the same time,
I wished there was something I wanted
As badly as he wanted to fry himself.

I do not know how badly you want to see the church close its generational gap, rise from its current plateau, and move boldly into the future. But it will take wanting it badly enough to effect the kind of change necessary to make a difference.

Principle 3
Be as conciliatory as possible on unimportant details.

Some things are worth dying for, while others are not. Do not change anything that does not have to be changed. Give in on as many nonessential points as possible, conceding that there are several possible variables within the context of the multi-congregation church.

Acts 15 records that this was the spirit of the Jerusalem Conference. The apostles and elders who attended wanted to nail down essentials, but were willing to be conciliatory on as many minor points as possible. It was in this spirit of expediency that Paul circumcised Timothy, whose father was a Greek (Acts 16:1–3). The wise apostle knew that this symbolic bow to old tradition would make the young disciple's work among the Jews more effective.

I talked to a pastor one time about a fight that was brewing in his church. "What is the problem?" I asked. He told me, "I have a couple of boxes I want to store at the church, and the deacons do not think that is appropriate." (What strange things church fights are made of!) My advice was to back off, to take the boxes home for storage there.

Choose the hills you are going to fight on carefully, and ask yourself, "Is this worth dying for?" If not, get off the hill. Some pastors believe that to back down on *any* point will call their authority into question. I have found the opposite to be true. If you show yourself willing to give in and be flexible on unimportant issues, people will be more likely to be flexible on the things that really matter to you. On the other hand, if you insist on getting your way every time, you position yourself as stubborn, rigid, and immature.

Suppose, as pastor, you want to launch a new service for young adults. You think it should be on Saturday night. Everyone else thinks Sunday at 9:45 A.M. would be better. I would acquiesce. Keep the big point of having a new service and let the others tinker with the schedule. Obviously, if they were suggesting a schedule that was just not workable, that is another matter, but give on as many points as possible.

Principle 4
Provide ample opportunity for open discussion.

As a leader, you must allow time for ideas involving change to be digested, for the body to hear from each other and for you to receive their feedback. A healthy mind needs time to make a U-turn. Pressure the maneuvering and you will all be in the ditch.

Notice in Acts 6:1–7 how the church handled its first fight—a conflict about food distribution. The Twelve called everyone together. The text does not record every detail of the meeting, but it does give us the idea that this was a town meeting, a public, open discussion. The solution arrived at "pleased the whole group" (v. 5).

When we have important matters to bring before our church membership, we will often schedule a "Family Forum." Since these meetings have no formal authority, there is no vote taken, no action, no motions, and often no agenda. We leaders just want to hear from the body. And we want the parts of the body to listen to each other. One of the innate problems with the multi-congregation church is that communication is more difficult than in a traditional arrangement. Family Forums help to bridge that. We have found that change is more acceptable if it has been openly discussed by all those concerned, rather than being handed down as a mandate from the leadership.

If you want to speed the rate of change, says Schaller, "increase the number and frequency of discussion, both formal and informal, about the proposed course of action. Most changes require a quantity of talk or 'milling around,' and the time span for fulfilling this requirement often can be shortened, thus accelerating the pace of change."[7]

Another principle we try to follow is based on the observation that people normally do their best thinking about a new idea on the drive home from the meeting where it is discussed (and in the shower the next morning). Therefore, in important matters, we try to bring forward plenty of information before the meeting, then have the discussion, and make the decision at a follow-up meeting. People hate to feel that they are being ramrodded. They need more time and space to make a free decision. If leaders cannot spare that time, it is probably an indication that some skill development in project management is needed on their part.

Principle 5
Use written documents to persuade the left-brained.

Notice that the Jerusalem Conference issued a formal statement (Acts 15:22–29). A letter was drafted, with careful wording describing the outcome. I get the feeling that the specific language of the letter was approved by a "committee" of leaders. The more controversial a matter is, the more this is necessary. When wading into controversy, we have found it helps to cover every detail. This is not necessary if everyone is getting along and is in agreement. But when there is potential conflict, move down into a writing mode. Draft a written proposal that outlines the course of action. This document will have an air of formality and authority if it is issued jointly by the ordained and lay leaders of the church. It should also serve as a record of what was decided.

115

Principle 6
Use storytelling to persuade the right-brained.

Most people are right-brained. You may not win them with logic, but you will probably win them with stories, which is why I told you about "Unchurched Harry" in chapter 1.

When Peter was asked by the Jews about the conversion of Cornelius and the other early Gentile believers, he recounted everything that had happened. He told a story, rather than argue the theology of the acceptance of the Gentiles (Acts 11:1–18). Paul told the story of his conversion on three separate occasions. Stories sell better than abstract philosophizing.

Yes, talk about concepts and ideas. But do not refrain from telling stories of churches that have attempted building programs that did not work. They are easy to find. On the positive side, tell stories of real flesh-and-blood individuals whose lives are being changed by the gospel.

Mandy came in the office the other day with a problem. She had been born again about three weeks earlier. Prior to that she had been on drugs and had a self-described alcohol problem, as well as a promiscuous lifestyle. That was B.C., before Christ came into her life. Recently some Christians had been telling her of the importance of having a quiet time. They advised her to get a spiritual journal to record both her prayer requests and the answers. But Mandy preferred to pray in the shower and was worried about getting her notebook all wet. She had come to see one of her pastors to ask if it was all right to pray in the shower. She was dead serious.

Stories like that thrill me because they are so fresh, like the innocent but profound things children say.

Telling true stories about the effect Christ is having on people's lives is far more influential than reciting dry, logical arguments. Concepts, reasoning, statistics, and graphs are helpful, but stories do 90 percent of the persuading. Tell stories like Mandy's and then say we need to adopt the multi-congregational model so more people like her will come to faith in Jesus.

Principle 7
Be as open with information as possible.

Do not hide anything. If you do not know all the facts, say so. Trust the Lord and be honest with his people. Do not treat them like worms, keeping them in the dark and feeding them manure.

I am impressed by how open Peter was about the Cornelius experience, and I admire Paul's candor at the Jerusalem Conference.

Hidden agendas will destroy your credibility with the membership. Tell them everything you are thinking. Share your dreams, your expectations, even your doubts.

Principle 8
Expect opposition to change.

The most natural, normal, predictable reaction to change is anger or fear—or both. I am always surprised at how seasoned pastors who should know better will be blind-sided by the resistance to change that is typical of most human beings. The Book of Acts records many instances where the early church's leaders experienced regular and frequent opposition to change. It did not surprise them, and it should not surprise you.

Principle 9
Confront when necessary.

Paul tells the story of a time he had to confront Peter, who had been eating openly with Gentiles *until* some friends from Jerusalem came to town. Then he went back to his exclusionary behavior. Paul nailed him on this point: "You are

117

dead wrong, Peter, and you are distorting and denying the gospel you preach. Straighten up" (Gal. 2:11, my paraphrase). There comes a time for speaking out boldly.

Principle 10
Concentrate on what God has called you to do: growing a church.

Paul confronted change when he needed to do so. Church leaders wrote documents and told stories when that was necessary. They discussed when they needed to discuss. But, *most of the time,* they just kept preaching Jesus. Richard Jackson, former pastor of North Phoenix Baptist Church, says his father taught him that people will forgive a lot of things if you preach well and keep the baptistry water disturbed each week.

Pour as much quality time as possible into what gets results. Spend just enough "political" time to implement your efforts.

Principle 11
Realize you must spend some time on unpleasant tasks.

Every job has things we enjoy and things that are unpleasant. I once heard a former minister say that he would get back into the ministry if it were not for "the politics." I choose to put up with the politics and other annoyances so I can enjoy the other 90 percent of my professional life.

I do not think Paul enjoyed attending the Jerusalem Conference. He would rather have been out preaching Jesus and planting churches. But he knew he should "go up to Jerusalem to see the apostles and elders" and tell them about God's work among the Gentiles (Acts 15:2, 12). Failure to convince the council on this point would jeopardize his opportunity at Ephesus, Philippi, and Corinth. We must ask God to give us the wisdom to balance all aspects of our calling.

Principle 12
Pray constantly for the coming of the kingdom.

Peter Wagner says that the more he studies church planting and church growth, the deeper he is convicted that very profound issues of spiritual warfare are involved: "The more deeply I dig beneath the surface of church growth principles, the more thoroughly convinced I become that the real battle is a spiritual battle and that our principal weapon is prayer."[8] As Elisha prayed that his servant would be able to see into the unseen world (2 Kings 6:17), we too need to pray that God will allow us to recognize the specific forces of evil that are undermining the work of God. "Resist the devil, and he will flee from you" (James 4:7).

The Book of Acts contains many references to prayer (e.g., 1:14; 2:42; 6:4; 16:13), and no doubt the petitioning of those early Christians often included the phrase "Thy kingdom come," which the Lord had taught them. As we work toward necessary changes within the church, we must pray constantly for the coming of the kingdom, for then we are asking God for at least three things:

- That the lost will continue to accept the king
- That babes in Christ will grow to spiritual maturity
- That God will change the hard hearts of those who stand in the way of the advancement of his kingdom

In all our strivings, we need to recognize that apart from Christ we can do nothing (John 15:5). When God blesses and allows change to take place—when we see the outpouring of his spirit and the fulfillment of our prayers as hundreds of people come to faith in Christ—we need to cultivate our awareness of why this happened. "'Not by might nor by power, but by my Spirit,' says the LORD Almighty" (Zech. 4:6). As our staff prays together, we regularly confess that without the Lord we are powerless. At the same

119

time, we confess our strong confidence that with God all things are possible, that we will be given whatever we ask in Christ's name (John 15:16).

Principle 13
Meet the real needs of everyone.

I once had a conversation with someone who said, "People will be opposed to the multi-congregation church because they are used to a one-on-one relationship with their pastor. When they come to church, he is there. When they need help, he is there. He marries their children and buries their dead. He is there when they are in the hospital." This man was saying that members of a congregation expect their varied and ongoing personal needs to be met by their church leaders in some tangible way. It follows that so long as they have some assurance that these needs will continue to be met, they will be more open to changes in *how* they are met.

A leader must have the insight to look behind a spoken request to get at the real need and then work at meeting that need. We can find an example of this principle in Acts 6:1–7. It would have been easy enough for the Twelve to hear the complaints of the Grecian widows and then preach a sermon on "Do everything without complaining or arguing." That would not fix the basic problem. The real issue was not food distribution. It was a problem rooted in prejudice and inadequate pastoral care, a situation that had arisen because the apostles were stretching themselves too thin—trying to handle both the ministry of the word of God and the care of the needy. The early church solved this problem by appointing seven men to take over the responsibility for the material needs of its members, and "this proposal pleased the whole group" (Acts 6:5).

Every personal problem is not caused by a spiritual deficiency. Some are evidence of real needs. Wise is the leader who knows the difference. In the multi-congregation church, as in every large church, some organized system of lay pastoral care must be implemented. When real needs are being met, people will be far more likely to allow you to start as many services as you want!

Principle 14
Maintain integrity.

Paul's statement in Acts 24:16 has always been one of my favorite texts: "So I strive always to keep my conscience clear before God and man." No one has ever been able to improve on Bill Gothard's definition of a clear conscience: "Being able to say, 'No one can point a finger at me and say, "You wronged me and never tried to make it right."'"9

Oh, how easy it is to forget this. When in the middle of a battle you know to be important, it is easy to rationalize that the ends justify the means. But the kingdom of God is not advanced through anything less than sterling-silver honesty and integrity.

I will detail in a later chapter a few of the wrong things I have done. I am painfully aware that I have hurt people in a profound way, and I stand in a posture of repentance toward these things. By the way, if you struggle with this, I suggest you get in the habit of saying, "I was wrong" every day, just to stay in practice.

Is there anyone you have wronged and need to talk to? Clear your conscience before God and man: Make it right and ask for forgiveness.

7

Corollaries for Change Agents

In addition to the fourteen principles on change found in the Book of Acts, there are nine related corollaries—inferences I have drawn from my own ongoing experience as a "change agent."

Corollary 1
Use the pulpit fully but fairly.

Cast your vision before the people in nearly every message, but be able to demonstrate that the vision comes directly off the pages of Scripture. If you are doing an expository study, you should have found pieces of the vision on every page and not be hesitant about pointing them out.

I confess that I have sometimes blown this principle. One time this happened was when I was functioning as interim pastor, as well as applying to be pastor (more about that in chapter 10). I was preaching through the Book of Acts on Sunday nights. I got to Stephen's address and concluded after careful study that the "big idea" of the passage was that God's people have often missed God's man. Israel missed Moses by not recognizing him as their deliverer, the brothers missed Joseph's significance, and so on. I still think that is a legitimate interpretation of the passage. There was, however, this heavy implication that the church members were missing their star candidate as pastor, though he was right under their noses. It was a stupid time to preach that sermon!

The point is this: Be cautious about using the Bible to support what is perceived to be a particular political view in the church, especially when it is anything less than straightforward, direct teaching from Scripture. It may be legitimate to preach from a certain text in neutral circumstances, but it will not be received well in volatile environments.

In other words, suppose you are preaching from Paul's testimony: "I have become all things to all men . . ." (1 Cor. 9:22). You do your research and conclude that the "big idea" is that we ought to be willing to do anything short of sin to reach people for Christ. That is a fairly straightforward application of the text. But it is another matter to take the next step and say that this verse compels the church to start a Saturday-night service. Starting a Saturday-night service might be one application of this idea, but the text does not *demand* that we do so. It only demands a "whatever it takes" attitude. When you cross the line of impartiality, people will see it and resent it. If you are not sure, err on the side of not being "political." You will always have next week to hit the vision again. If you try to manipulate Scripture so that it appears to endorse your own pet programs, you will lose the respect of your audience. Take it from me, that is very hard to gain back. The mistake of some visionaries is getting too far in front of the populace, pushing for too much change too fast and thereby sacrificing their opportunity to influence the group on the ultimate goals.

The best way to influence the thinking of the church body is by presenting a solid, structured, consistent demonstration from the pulpit that there is a sound scriptural basis for the vision you are casting before them. Use as many specific prooftexts as you can, but be sure they are truly relevant. Above all, proceed slowly but steadily, skillfully but impartially.

Corollary 2
Tame your tongue.

Don't say anything that you would not want heard by everyone—because it probably will. Just when you think you know who your friends are, who you can let your hair down with, one of them will bite you. But you can relax about that if you stay with saying only kind things about people. Then you will not have to worry about having them repeated.

Corollary 3
Expect God to come through for you.

Never forget that we are in spiritual business with a living God who can work miracles.

Remember the time Paul was shipwrecked on Malta and bitten by a snake? *God came through.*

Remember the time Moses faced an ocean in front of him and an army behind him? *God came through.*

Remember the time Daniel was on the lion's menu? *God came through.*

Remember Abraham, Joseph, Gideon, Elijah, and all the others in the ranks of faith? *God came through.*

God has come through for me in unbelievable ways, more often than I could count, but I particularly remember one of the greatest challenges in my ministry. One Friday morning I received a message from the church secretary asking me to preach all services that weekend. Further investigation revealed that my sermon would immediately follow the announcement of the pastor's resignation. What do you say in a time like that? You say what God gives you. I have never felt as clearly led to say anything. Just as Jesus said it would happen, God came through.

Corollary 4
Be alert and responsive to rumors.

Unfortunately, pastors are not always privy to what is really going on in the church. Pastors could put a plaque on their desk that reads, "The grapevine stops here." People just do not tell us everything directly, so we are insulated from the real scoop.

It is for this reason that we must deal proactively with rumors and establish a feedback system to keep informed. When you casually get wind that so-and-so doesn't like this-or-that, do not let it lie. You have probably just touched the tip of the iceberg.

In our church, the deacons are a very reliable sounding board for this kind of thing. Because we have a rotating system and the deacons are elected by popular vote, they are very "close to the customer." They are an accurate sample of the church as a whole, with the exception that they are all leaders, thoroughly churched, and do not always have a lot of sensitivity to the view of the outsider or the fringe person. But, in terms of keeping us out of trouble, they are terrific.

Because our Saturday-night service uses a contemporary format, we always have quite a number of people on the stage, and it is advantageous to move the pulpit to make more room. Our pulpit is a monster that must weigh at least 6,000 pounds. It is a rock. It requires two Herculean men and plenty of grunts and groans to move it, and they were doing that twice each weekend.

So, one Sunday morning, I asked Sam, "Do you think anyone would care if we just left this thing down here?"

"I don't know. Let's try it and see," he said.

We tried it and did not hear a thing for weeks. We thought all was well. Oh, we heard a person or two say something like, "You know, pastor, it does not bother me personally, but I hear there are others. . . ." We ignored it.

Dumb.

A real good course of action at this point would have been to investigate, to take it to the deacons and say, "This is what we have heard. Have *you* heard anything?" After that, unless we became aware that this was an issue that bothered quite a number of people, it would have become deacon-approved policy. Wow! "Deacon-approved policy" is much better than a "loose-cannon-on-deck decision" by the staff.

As it was, we ignored the problem until there was a big blowup.

Some things are worth fighting for. Moving a pulpit is not one of them, even a three-ton pulpit. If I am going to fight, I want to make sure that the issue is worth the potential loss. But I cannot know that until I get a reading of how the body feels. Because I know I am insulated, I must be alert and responsive to rumors. People are often intimidated by the pastor because of his title or his manner. This thickens his insulation from the grapevine and makes it necessary for him to investigate every hint of unrest.

Corollary 5
Honor every long-standing tradition.

John Maxwell is a master at this. If you listen to him speak of Pastor Orval Butcher, the founding pastor whom he succeeded, you would think he was talking about the apostles Peter and Paul rolled into one.[1]

And for good reason. Pastor Butcher did many good things.

But the truth is, Skyline Wesleyan Church had been plateaued for some time when John Maxwell arrived. You could well argue that although Pastor Butcher had taken the church as far as he could, change needed to take place. It is John Maxwell who put this church on the map. It is John Maxwell who made it famous. It is John Maxwell who made it great.

Perhaps John Maxwell should talk about only the things that have happened since John Maxwell arrived on the scene, but John Maxwell is smarter than that. Rather than positioning himself in opposition to Pastor Butcher's policies, he has characterized himself as fulfilling the lifelong dream that Pastor Butcher wanted for this church. That is incredibly smart. Change management will go more smoothly if past, present, and future are seen as a continuum—an ongoing and direct pathway to what God has purposed.

Sit down with some of your long-standing old-guard types. Ask them about the history of your church. Ask them why the founders wanted to start this church in the first place. Ask them why they wanted these buildings and why they sacrificed to keep the doors open. Collect some good stories. Then point out how past growth, the current way of doing things, and the proposed changes all represent fulfillment of those original dreams. If you can get some documentation and quote from it, so much the better. And do not do this just once or twice.

One legitimate need of all people is a sense of history. It gives us a sense of roots, a foundation on which to stand. Demonstrate to your members every instance where you are staying with their traditions. Point out, for example, that this is the fourteenth *annual* Fourth of July picnic. Especially if you are a newcomer to the church staff, you may not be thinking of picnics as part of your strategy for change. However, pointing out that this particular picnic has long been an annual event—and will therefore be retained on the church calendar—will be very important to many in the congregation. Honoring the past can lend stability to any journey into the future.

Corollary 6
Build better freeways, not tow trucks.

I once attended a conference in El Paso that was held on the top floor of a tall hotel building. The conference was a bust, but while looking out the window during lunch, I had a serendipitous thought that was worth the whole trip.

The hotel overlooks I-10, which was buzzing with cars. Just watching all that even-flowing movement inspired me to think, "My problem is, I am relying on tow trucks instead of clearly marked roads that lead to a desirable destination. I tend to drag people where *I* want them to go, rather than providing freeways so inviting that they want to go there, too."

Mark it well, the difference between a multi-congregation church and a traditional one is not the number of services; it is the way church is perceived. Unless your people want to go there, you cannot tow enough of them with your wrecker. You must change their inclinations, and that is more profound than altering the schedule.

This is why my advice is to allow people time, give them things to read, tell them stories. But keep your goal in mind: a church with more services than it already has. You want your people saying to you, "Pastor, do you think we could launch another congregation this Easter?" They must own the plan. They have got to love it.

I am not naive as to how difficult this is. That is why I have said my vision is to give to the next generation a better way of doing church. I estimate it will take a whole generation to change the existing mind-set.

Corollary 7
Build trust through love.

I occasionally hear pastors talk about their church, their board, their deacons, this committee or that, as if they were the enemy. They certainly are not. The enemy is the devil, the world, and the flesh. Mental attitudes may need changing, but you will never do it without a deep and profound love. Doing it any other way would not be Christianity; it would be a great abuse of your authority. If you show people your love, they will trust you to look out for their interests.

"Focus attention," says Schaller, "not on the proposed change, but on building up the level of trust. The higher the level of trust, the easier it is for planned change to take place."[2]

Corollary 8
Get a support group.

People are influenced by facts. To a greater degree, they are influenced by storytelling and testimonies. But, mostly, they are influenced by their friends. You must not wave the flag alone. You need a group to help you hold it high. Talk a lot about your ideas being supported by these allies. Saying "I think we should do as Bob suggested" positions you as being far more reasonable than always insisting on having your own way.

The best way to build a support group is one on one, over a cup of coffee. Involve people in the early planning stages, while you are still deciding about the particulars. If you wait till you have made up your mind, it puts you into a salesman-customer relationship, which is basically adversarial. Get with them early and say, "Let's brainstorm about this. What if we launched a Saturday-night service?" We have learned the hard way that we tend not to bring forward ideas until they are well thought through—until we know this is something we want to do and are emotionally committed to it. This procedure gets in the sales mode. It is far better to try to move ideas early in the "just something to think about" stage.

Corollary 9
Quote the right sources.

If there is a well-respected and innovative church you can point to, preferably in your denomination, you are miles ahead. People have a fear of being first in the water; they want to know what is below the surface. I am that way. A builder told me he wanted to put a new kind of insulation in my house. He explained that it had been thoroughly tested, and he listed the advantages. My question was: "Am I the first?" If he could say, "Oh, no, I have put it in a dozen houses and the owners are all pleased," it would be far more persuasive than quoting a 900-page study by several major universities.

The key value here is the respect that your congregation has for the church you are using as an example. We have used Saddleback (Rick Warren's church in Mission Viejo) as an example of some things we want to do. For some, this is very impressive, since it is the fastest-growing, largest, and biggest contributor to the denomination in California. To others, Saddleback means little. You can tell because they like to make jokes about the name—"I don't want anything to do with 'Camel-snout,' or whatever that weird place is in California." If I hear such remarks too often, I know I have quoted the wrong source.

8

Moving Toward a
Multi-Congregation Model

In this chapter I want to get as specific as I can in outlining a path for the multi-congregational approach, although you will need to adjust the recipe to your own situation.

Start an 8:30 Worship Service on Sunday Morning

A traditional church that already has a service at 11:00 and a 9:45 Sunday school can start an 8:30 service with very little administrative hassle. (Starting a new service is much easier than starting a new Sunday school.) Although it might seem that all the pastor and staff would have to do is get up an hour earlier and line up musicians and ushers, you should have taken some of the following steps beforehand:

1. *Talk about the new service at least six to nine months before you start it.* Use lots of nonthreatening language like, "What if we . . . ?" and "What would it be like if someday . . . ?"

(Few people are opposed to doing anything "someday," even if they do not like the basic idea of changing. If it is a change "someday," they can live with that.)

2. *Write up a summary paper on why an early service might be a good idea.* Set it out on a table in the foyer and leave it there for several months. Give lots of facts, data, quotes, evidence, and stories, stories, stories.

3. *Cast a vision for the new service from the pulpit.* Demonstrate through Scripture how it would contribute to fulfilling the Great Commission.

4. *Allow various groups to talk about the idea.* Have the subject introduced in Sunday school and prayer groups and meetings of staff and lay leaders. Encourage everyone to express an opinion on the matter.

5. *Describe the venture as an "experiment," implying that the change need not be permanent.* Dr. Streeter credits much of the growth of the early church to this little word: "It is permissible to hint that the first Christians achieved what they did because the spirit with which they were inspired was one favorable to *experiment*."[1] People like having the assurance of a money-back guarantee, as many business organizations have found. Very few people take them up on the offer, and it is easier to sell the product.

6. *Get official approval at least three months prior to launching the service.* This gives plenty of time for people to get used to the idea. During this period, every newsletter ought to contain some reference to it, such as: "When we start that new service. . . ." Don't let the membership forget.

7. *Conduct an in-house survey to see who would be interested in moving to the alternate time.* Then design the service for this market group. Although your central purpose is outreach, you will need a core group from your existing membership to help establish the new congregation. Pastors tend to think they talk to enough people to have a good feel for the church as a whole, but this is usually not true. If you ask people to *write*

down their opinions about what they do and do not like about a proposal, it is amazing how revealing the answers will be.

8. *Do as much advertising for the new service as you can.* If money is tight but people are willing to volunteer, do a tele-marketing campaign, as we did to launch our Saturday-night service. Telemarketing is very effective, but it is also a tremendous amount of work. That is why we do not use this technique anymore. It is far easier (although more expensive) to do direct mail. However you do it, advertise for the new service on a broad scale. This is a wonderful opportunity to invite new people to your church, and it will really help to make the service a success. What we have found is that if we advertise one service, people will come to some of the others as well. (If you could send 200 pieces of mail for every seat in your auditorium, you are almost certain of success.) But printed advertising is tricky. Money is not the only factor—it must be done right. Sloppy adver-tising is counterproductive. The quality of paper, the art-work, and the words on the page send a message. Make sure it is the message you want sent.

9. *Consider an alternate music format.* Perhaps, for example, contemporary music might be a drawing card for young adults. One commentator writes: "The pipe organ is nearly as old as Western Civilization, but there is less and less for it to do in the modern suburban sanctuary, given the deep decline in membership of denominations that were the bas-tions of organ music—Presbyterians and Episcopalians, par-ticularly. At the same time, more and more churches are playing down classical religious music in favor of a 'Chris-tian top-40' sound."[2] You may also want to consider a coun-try format. Do some homework first:

- Visit a church that is adept at contemporary worship. A successful model is everything, especially with ref-erence to music.

- Rent (or buy) a good synthesizer and find someone who loves to play it or is willing to learn. A good synthesist has right-brained musicianship and left-brained computer skills and will transform the sound of your music. Instrumentation is what makes the difference. A bass guitar, drums, and other instruments can give a new feel to the music, but a good synth can do the job just as well.
- Get permission to copy. Christian Copyright Licensing, Inc. (CCLI) offers a competitively priced license to copy a broad selection of suitable music. Contact them at 6130 N.E. 78th Ct. Suite C-11, Portland, OR 97218. Or call 1-800-234-2446.
- Put together a small vocal band. Modern ears are not used to a large traditional choir and prefer the more familiar sound of individual voices. However, it is important that each singer be on pitch all the time! If someone is missing notes regularly, it is hard to cover up, because most small groups perform with microphones. Have the group begin rehearsals at least two months before the first service so they will have a stockpile of several weeks of material. (You will probably be doing six to ten songs a week.)
- Repeat some of the vocal music from one week to the next. Assume that the audience is initially unfamiliar with the songs but will learn them through repetition.

10. *If you decide to stay with the same music format, have the choir sing in the early service.* They might sing in the first service, attend Sunday school, sing in the early part of the second service, then leave while you greet one another. This way, the service is seen as first class.

11. *Have the regular pastor conduct the first additional service.* You cannot afford the perception that this is a second-class service. Preaching a sermon twice is a piece of cake and just

gets better with practice. There is also an inherent efficiency in not having two people preparing messages for the same day. The only exception to this rule is if there is *already* on staff an exceptionally popular pastor whose preaching style will attract a target group to the alternate time.

12. *Sit down with some of your most popular lay leaders and try to get them excited about the new service.* I cannot over-estimate how important it is to get influencers on your side. People move in groups and follow leaders they trust.

13. *Do a dress rehearsal the week before your first public service.* The purpose is to work the bugs out so you can do it right when your guests arrive.

Hire Additional Staff to Share the Pastoral Responsibilities

A church going the multi-congregational route needs depth and variety among its paid professionals. Although any new staff member will undoubtedly have other assignments besides preaching (education, administration, small groups, discipleship, and so on), four things should be true of a church with more than one preacher/pastor:

1. *All pastors should be equally competent in preaching.* If the senior pastor is far superior in this area, everyone will soon be aware that the new person is "second string." However, if only their *styles* are different, this can be a strength, since it will lessen the sense of competition that is so deadly to a multi-congregation (or multi-service) church.

2. *All pastoral staff members should share the same basic theology.* Two pastors with widely divergent theologies should not be preaching in the same church. (An Arminian and a Calvinist would have trouble sharing a pulpit!) But things will work fine so long as there are no clear-cut disagreements—for example, if you have both a strong dispensationalist and someone who is neutral on the subject. If minor

differences on doctrine are fairly acknowledged and even celebrated, the contrast in emphasis will strengthen the over-all ministry of the church. Preaching debates, on the other hand, will only divide and confuse the congregation.

3. *The staff must be together in terms of its philosophy of ministry.* I think this is more important than being in agreement over every jot and tittle of theology.

4. *Staff members need to have a gut-level trust in each other.* It is best if they can become really good friends who love to sip coffee together. This calls for a profound sense of mutual respect as well as sharing a team spirit. They ought to look forward to meetings and enjoy praying together. Even though the staff may not spend a lot of personal time together, there should be no reluctance to do so. It certainly helps if their families are compatible, too!

Launch a Worship Service or Study Group on a Day Other Than Sunday

This may be tougher to do than merely adding another service on Sunday. First of all, it may be harder to staff. Asking the needed personnel to get up one hour earlier on Sunday is far easier than getting them to operate on another day. This is particularly true with unpaid volunteers, many of whom have work schedules or family commitments that would make it difficult for them to come on, say, a weeknight or even a Saturday. For example, you may have to recruit an entirely new group of Bible-study teachers.

In addition, if you ask people to come on a new day, you must let them become accustomed to the change, especially if they are traditionalists who believe that church attendance must always be on Sunday. Be innovative, anyway, referring to the steps outlined above.

Instruct Your People on the Advantages and Goals of the Multi-Congregational Approach

By the time your church gets to three services, it is getting close to the maximum that one preacher can handle. Another paradigm shift will be necessary to take it farther along. Since this means discarding the traditional approach and picking up a new one, allow plenty of time to mull this over with key individuals. Over the course of several months, take them all to coffee, one on one, and discuss this with them. Your purpose is to listen to their ideas and feelings (especially their fears) and to explain what is meant by the multi-congregational approach. Be sure you have researched the subject enough to be able to speak with clarity and credibility.

A lady called our church office to complain that we had left the denomination. She had confused multi-congregational with unitarian church. Clarity will not come automatically.

This book could be one resource, but as you begin to look around, you will find magazine articles and other materials that speak to the subject. Recommend them to your membership, especially the lay leaders. If there are pertinent conferences in the area, take your key people along.

Provide Opportunities for Open Discussion

It is just as important that all your members talk to each other—in a formal way—as it is that leaders make speeches. People will talk anyway, but you want to make sure these conversations are more than the grapevine variety. There will probably be some groups that like the proposed change and others that do not. By allowing for public forums, you provide an opportunity for all views to be examined openly. This is much more persuasive than leader-to-congregation communication alone.

Of course, you must also have disseminated enough facts to ensure that these discussions are not merely rooted in raw emotions. One mistake many leaders make is believing that all important decisions are made in business conferences, committee meetings, and boardrooms. No. They are made over coffee at the breakfast bar and by housewives on the phone. If you are not dropping large volumes of accurate information into the circles of everyday conversation, you are lost. It was said of Martin Luther that one of the things that made him so successful as a change agent is that he kept the German people informed of what was happening and what he was doing at each stage.[3]

Expand Your Facilities at the Same Time You Expand the Number of Services

You cannot turn the ship on a dime. The older the church and the more established it is, the longer it will take to make changes. If too much is changed too soon, the pastor will be asked to leave also. Try to keep capital expenses within 15 percent of your budget. Fund-raising companies project that a budget can be matched for three years. A church that has a million dollar annual budget should be able to raise two to three million in three years. But that accomplishment normally kills the pastor and squelches the growth of the church. Keep your expansion projects manageable.

On the other hand, if services are multiplied without expansion of the facilities, sooner or later there will be trouble. There is a finite number of usable time slots in a week. Further, there is an inherent efficiency in large buildings. A pastor can preach to a thousand people as easily as one hundred.

Develop a Ten-Year (or Longer) Master Plan

Look into the future of your church. First project the number and types of services you expect to have added by several specified dates (using one- or two-year intervals). Then calculate the facilities and staff that will be needed to accommodate those plans. If you do not know how to use a spreadsheet,[4] this is a good time to learn. Once you sell your master plan, all the projected changes are built into "tradition."

Annual decisions add additional services. Big dreams and carefully thought-through plans tend to attract the kind of people that can help you make it happen. Sloppy plans and vague ideas only breed chaos. Your master plan will also identify problem points when the system is getting out of balance.

We try to plan to have 65 percent occupancy as our total capacity. This is lower than the traditional 80 percent rule, because you can never keep multiple congregations evenly balanced. It is far easier to make adjustments in size of staff, size of buildings, and number of services on a spreadsheet than to deal with a crisis caused by poor planning. If you suddenly discover that you need a bigger building, more staff, and more services *all at the same time,* you are in trouble. (An example of a master plan is seen in Appendix B.)

Once the document is in place, many future decisions have already been made and unofficially approved. For example, your plan specifies that within two years the church will have launched two new worship services (early Sunday morning and Wednesday evening), a Tuesday-morning prayer meeting, and a support group for seniors on Friday afternoon. The data on your spreadsheet indicates that (1) one more staff person must be hired to implement those programs and (2) there is no need to expand the facilities, since there is available space in the building complex in those time slots. Of course, no master plan is etched in stone. Changing needs in the community may require you to revise your projections of what additional services may be needed by a given date. And experience may have shown you that the formulas you have used to determine personnel and space requirements are flawed. Nevertheless, as successful businesses have discovered, long-range planning is the most efficient way to accomplish broad objectives.

Your master plan will be meaningless and impractical if it has been arbitrarily laid down by a few church leaders. To get the entire membership behind it, you must gather wide input during the planning stage, encourage broad-based dialogue, and obtain both formal and grass-roots approval of the final document. Only if there is consensus among the people who will be affected will they claim ownership of the church's future and cooperate to make the plan workable.

Realize That You Cannot Change Everything

You cannot lead people where they do not want to go, which is not such a bad thing. Think about it. If a person of clearly non-Christian beliefs came into your church and tried to work these principles of change into his own agenda, it is likely he would not be successful. You can be confident of that and be glad. No matter how carefully he communicated, how slowly he moved, or how clever he was, he would probably convince only a few. People will not tolerate changes that threaten their basic beliefs and values. Similarly, you would probably not be able to change a Baptist church into a Presbyterian church. It is this reality that George Barna is speaking about when he writes, "The fact is that it *is* substantially easier to start fresh than to recast an existing body into a new entity."[5] It is for this reason that many of the multi-congregation churches that will dot America in the year 2010 will have been started *after* 1995.

9

Suggestions for Church Planters

If you want to have a multi-congregation church, it is easier if you start out that way. Then you will not have to make the massive paradigm shifts mentioned in the previous chapters. This has some important implications for church planters.

Work Closely with Sponsors

A church planter normally has a relatively free hand in shaping the nature of the church, but how much freedom he has depends on the sponsorship arrangement. A self-supported church planter can do almost anything he wants. Of course, he has to live with the consequences. If a denomination and/or other sponsoring body is involved, the rules are a little different. Money imparts power and influence and the right to control.

For this reason, I suggest that a church planter be as open as possible about every detail of his work. People do not like surprises. They are naturally suspicious of the unfamiliar. If you are involved in launching a new church, you may want to give your sponsors a copy of this book so they understand the philosophy behind what you are doing.

We planted a church—actually two churches—on the east side of Las Cruces. The sponsoring committee envisioned it as more or less a multi-congregation church from the very beginning—one English-speaking congregation and one for those of Hispanic background. There has been some tension between the two groups living in the same house, but none with the sponsors.

There are two issues at stake here. The first is integrity. It is dishonest and wrong to try to create a multi-congregation church without the knowledge of the parent body or against the will of the nominal sponsor. The other issue is more practical. Not only is it wrong; it is dumb. You will not be able to hide the fact that you have five services and two preaching pastors.

Sometimes there is one group (or more) that serves as the sponsoring unit and another that comprises the core group for the new congregation. It is important to talk to both groups. Do not assume they see eye to eye. I have known a case where the church planter came to complete agreement with the sponsors, but never talked to the core group that had already formed under another pastor's leadership. It was disaster. The planter had envisioned a very contemporary church, and the sponsors were very open to that idea. But the core group was made up of several denominational employees who expected a more traditional approach. Not a pretty sight, although it did result in two church plantings instead of just one.

Begin with More Than One Regular Preacher

Remember, if you are ever going to be a multi-congregation church, you need to be one as early as possible. This means that *during the first quarter,* you need at least a second preacher in the pulpit on other than a substitutionary basis. Whatever you establish as the norm will be your "tradition" from then on. (At least, this is usually true.) A church in Roswell, New Mexico, started out with two pastors. Each had the serendipitous dual gifts of being able to preach and lead music. From the beginning, they have alternated their ministries: preaching one week and doing the music the next. Moving to the multi-congregation model will be a piece of cake for them.

If a church cannot start with two or more professionals who can preach, do not overlook laypeople. There is real potential here. If the body of Christ could find a way to train its lay leaders to communicate the gospel effectively from the pulpit, there would be no limit to church growth. Consider how much easier it would be for a pastor to develop three good sermons a quarter than to produce two or three a week, week after week. It is a very reasonable expectation that someone other than an official pastor will be able to preach three or four top-notch series a year. There would be twelve weeks in between time to gather illustrations and polish the messages. Our church is just now getting into this experiment, and we are very optimistic about its end results.

Make It Your Aim to Get Over 200 Members as Quickly as Possible

The longer a church remains below the 200 mark, the greater the likelihood that it will continue to attract people who *prefer* a small church. Then growth will be difficult to achieve. Schaller points out that unless a church breaks the 200 barrier rather quickly, it is unlikely that it ever will. His recommendation is that church planters make it their goal to be above 200 on the very first weekend and never dip below that number.[1] People can keep a church small if they want to.

Advertising can help get the church above 200, as we saw in chapter 4. Part of doing this is simply a function of math. If you can get 20,000 high-quality flyers mailed, you have a good shot at attracting at least 200 first-time visitors. If you do a good job with the service, a good number will come back—125 is a reasonable expectation. With quality services and regular punches with advertising, a church can have above 200 members in rather short order.

The other side of this has nothing whatever to do with math. God can shut us down if we are too dependent on statistical probabilities. There is a fine line between being practical and wise and being so self-assured that we fail to depend on God. Jesus said, "I am the vine; you are the branches. If a man remains in me and I in him, he will bear much fruit; apart from me you can do nothing" (John 15:5).

My father used to pose a question to seminary students: "True or false?—'We can accomplish very little without abiding in Christ.'" There is only one right answer to that question: *False.* Most of us would like to believe we can do at least a *little* bit without abiding in Christ. We think we can do some good, even if we are not quite as spiritual as we ought to be. But Jesus taught that it was all or nothing. Advertising might draw a crowd, but it will never build the true church of God. True spiritual leaders recognize that the real life-changing work is not done through the mail, but on a person-to-person level, and *always* under God's direction.

One other note: Whatever you start with is what you tend to attract. Rick Warren was offered some people whose beliefs were very different from those of the church he was planting. He gave a polite "No, thank you." It takes keen perception and a great deal of faith to insist on a similar philosophy of ministry when a church has empty pews.

Begin with Several Staff Persons

It is often cheaper and more effective in the long run to start with more than one pastor.[2] Try to begin with as many qualified professionals as you can afford. Starting with a team allows the church to take off quickly and gain synergy and momentum from its own growth. On the other hand, if a church is slow-growing because of understaffing, it will have difficulty attracting the kind of visionary personalities that will fuel its growth in coming years. It will hover at a subsidy level for months and even years. Much better if sufficient fuel is provided to get it off the launching pad quickly.

Having more than one pastor allows several groups to form. Because you almost want to discourage that "family feeling" in the early days, try to cultivate a number of age- or interest-related groups immediately. If you are not occasionally accused of being cliquish, you are not doing a good job of this. If your objective is a multi-congregation church, you need to be working toward this model all along. With adequate staff available, you can start with more than one service, and more than one musical style. This is almost certain to begin the mosaic that is characteristic of a multi-congregation church.

Plan Facilities Around the Multi-Congregation Approach

Multi-congregation churches work best when their physical plant has been designed to house back-to-back ministries, allowing both sides of the building—education and worship—to be full at the same time. More space than in a traditional church will be needed in the nursery because both sides are being used. More rest rooms and parking space will be needed, as will ample foyers to ease the tension when services run longer than expected. Wide hallways will allow

147

people to move in two directions without feeling like they are being herded in a cattle drive. Furthermore, if we want them to stop and fellowship, the hall has to be wide enough to do so. The quicker and more easily people can move from one place to another, the better. (High schools are good examples of this idea.) In the Sun Belt, this space for movement could be provided through covered outdoor paths and landscaped patios. This is not only cheaper; it is more aesthetically pleasing—except in January.

Thought should be given to providing a place for musicians to warm up before each service. This needs to be sound-insulated from any adjacent educational and worship space. There should also be easy access to the auditorium or sanctuary. Our pastor does not require that musicians and staff listen to the sermon more than once, but we usually are present at the beginning or end of each service. For this reason, an unobtrusive entrance to the auditorium is helpful.

Because flexibility is a key value for the multi-congregation church, it should be reflected in the building design. There may come a time when you want to have several worship services going simultaneously—offering people a choice of topics and/or preachers and/or musical style without disrupting the small-group structure. Multi-unit movie theaters have been offering this kind of variety for years. On the other hand, the main auditorium of a multi-congregation church can actually be smaller than normal, since the goal is to use it often. It will be a big advantage if there are ways to adjust the actual number of seats in the auditorium, which will allow you to make maximum use of the space when necessary. When a new service is added, you can reduce the seating to avoid that rattling-in-a-big-room feeling.

Land requirements for a multi-congregation church are similarly reduced, as compared to a traditional church of the same total membership. For example, a church aspiring to accommodate all of its 1,000 members in only one or two services would need about seven acres for its building complex and parking space (see chapter 4: "Major expenses can be predicted"). If that same church were to hold several more services a week, and not always on Sunday, it could manage with more compact facilities, and therefore less acreage, at least so long as its membership remains at the 1,000-member level.

Make Decisions About Sunday School

There is some talk that on-site Sunday school is being replaced by home groups, since the warmer atmosphere is more "user friendly" to outsiders, and there is relatively unlimited space available. The downside is the difficulty of providing quality education for children in a multi-age family. Dr. John Vaughan has done some research on this and found the facts rather startling. Apparently, churches with a formal Sunday-school system do a far better job of assimilating people in some kind of group life than do churches with only a home-cell system. Independent, noncharismatic churches using home cells average 500 out of 1,000 worship attendees in small group activities. Independent, charismatic churches have about 300 in such groups. Those that employ a Sunday-school system, however, have from 750 and upward of those attending worship involved also in smaller group activities.[3]

However, the savings in the home system are enormous. As noted in chapter 4, a church should provide about ten square feet of auditorium space per person, whereas education requires about forty square feet per person. And a children's Sunday school requires more space than one for adults, who usually sit in straight rows in their classes. If they sit in one loop around the perimeter of the room they can waste a good deal of usable space.

The point is, there are advantages and disadvantages for both the home-group approach and traditional Sunday school. There has been no clear-cut evidence that a church is able to do *both* effectively over a long period of time. When launching a new church, you will need to decide which way you want to go. But choose your route carefully—it may be hard to turn back.

Expect to Do Some Fund Raising Every Year

Willow Creek is a good model for many aspects of church life. One thing it does well is fund raising. The leadership sends a couple of letters toward the end of every year, asking people to consider giving an amount above their tithe to building expansion. Because this is done every year, it is never a huge expenditure. Capital fund-raising goals should stay below 20 percent of the total budgeted giving. Most people like to give to buildings and are willing to do so annually, in amounts that do not strain their own budgets.

10

Our Story

No one planned that we would become a multi-congregation church. It just happened.

We grew, ran out of space, and started another service. We grew some more, ran out of space again, and started still another service. Then we added a Sunday school, another service, another Sunday school, and we added a service. . . .

Somewhere along the line, we started wondering if the model we had stumbled onto might not be more effective than the traditional approach. It was about this juncture that I had the quiet time described in the introduction. Many of the thoughts about the early church hit me that morning. Many of the principles on change were learned because we had violated them. Our successes taught us a few more.

I did not want to write this chapter. It seemed awfully egotistical to tell our story and much more reasonable merely to talk about principles and suggestions. But then I realized that when I attend conferences by people like Rick Warren, I sometimes want to say, "Cut the talk and get to the real stuff. What really happened?"

So, here is what really happened, warts and all. This is not a comprehensive history of our church, but rather the story of how we changed from a traditional church toward the multi-congregational model of Calvary Baptist Church.

I feel even more awkward in the sections of this chapter where I talk about myself like Linus when he said to Snoopy, "I am tired of talking about me. . . . *You* talk about me for a while." But once again, when I reflect on people I have learned from, I get interested not only in the theories, but also in the people who embody those theories.

There is another reason I did not want to write this chapter. As long as I stuck with theory and rhetoric, I could keep you believing nice things about me. You are about to discover the truth.

I grew up of missionary parents and lived my early years in the Philippines. I suppose this alone will help you understand my conservative bias toward spending. I grew up in a land where people live on garbage heaps and dig through the rubble to eke out a living (if you call that living), where little children did not wear pants until they started school. "Need" has a different definition in that context.

I remember coming back to the States, looking into the eyes of a grocery-store clerk in New York City, and thinking, "Do you have any idea how fortunate you are to live in this country? Do you think about drinking Dr. Pepper, eating Doritos, and enjoying all the amenities of American life? Do you have a clue what a privilege it is?"

I remember, too, panning my eyes slowly around the inside of an "average American" county-seat First Church auditorium. The contrast with what I had seen in the Philippines was unbelievable. And that is okay. I understand. If we are going to reach a particular people, we must do so in buildings that fit with their culture. But we must also use those buildings more than we do. It is sinful to waste them.

I am not preaching at you. I am telling you what I feel in the core of my being.

Enough of me. Let me tell you about our church. In many ways we are not yet a truly multi-congregation church. We are somewhere between multi-service and multi-congregation. So this book is not so much about what we *are* as it is about what we want to be. And I am looking for many people to come along with us.

I cannot overemphasize how right I feel about this journey. Never before have I seen the Bible, experience, and logic corroborate each other so harmoniously. I want to give to my sons a generation of churches that can do what God has put in all our hearts the passion to do—really make a difference in the world. May they see in their time the fulfillment of our prayer: "Your kingdom come, your will be done on earth as it is in heaven." I pray that every day.

Calvary's Past

Calvary is a typical forty-year-old "established" church. It was birthed through a planned-parenthood process in the early 1950s. The Women's Missionary Union (WMU) at First Baptist Church was the initiating force behind the mission. Land was purchased one block off the main street and, predictably, the church struggled to grow. Inexpensive land is not always a bargain. Not that those were bad days for the church. It just did not grow very much.

A few statistics from those early days provide insight into the early days of the church:

- In 1952, seventeen business meetings were held, one specially called to approve the purchase of a $13 sign.
- In January of 1952, Calvary's total gifts for the month of January were $219.

153

- In 1957, the church borrowed $48,000 to build a 40' × 100' auditorium.
- By 1962, Calvary was becoming a real church. It had fourteen standing committees!
- Total gifts for 1963 were $19,718, but the church had to forgo twenty-two needed pews that year because of debt.

Some farsighted people began to eye some land closer to the university and on a main thoroughfare. The church bought eight acres and sold the back four. (Who would ever need more than four acres?) The cost of this relocation in 1966 was $132,850. Bonds were issued to raise the money. In 1966, total gifts were $23,220; bond payments were $13,845. Income jumped 28 percent that year, but there was still $2,567.79 in unpaid bills. By 1969, gifts rose to $28,300, but bond payments took a third of this. This is an example of the financial struggle that restricts church planting and church growth: Money needed for program development is not available because it is being spent on the building.

The times just after the relocation proved to be very difficult days for Calvary. Financial difficulties nearly crippled its operation. Stories still circulate of the days when Treasurer Rodney Moore paid the light bill out of his own pocket, just to keep the place going. That was the spirit of the church: Do what it takes to survive. Again, despite the financial problems, some visionary leaders had the foresight to build and thereby provide more space. This vision prepared for the future, but cost heavily in the present.

By 1974, gifts to the church had risen to $61,632—double the amount raised five years earlier. Calvary was also out of space again and borrowed an additional $65,000 to provide more room for education.

Treasurer Rodney Moore writes of these difficult days:

For some eight or ten years at 1800 S. Locust the Church was burdened financially with the high cost of long term debt service. Not much was available for program activities. When we worked out of that all areas of the church life prospered . . . God is blessing like no other time in history.

The combination of a favorable location, adequate facilities, and a good pastor allowed the church to break through the "200 barrier." As the church grew, the debt was eventually paid off, making it possible to add additional staff—me! Cliff Ennen was the pastor who led the church in those days (1980). Cliff will always have a special place in my heart because he was my first pastor after seminary. Allow me to pay him tribute. He has gone to be with the Lord.

My wife had attended this church when she was in college and had always dreamed of going back to Las Cruces and to Calvary. When she became ill during my seminary days, I decided to make a trip to Las Cruces to ask for a job. "I would never dream of hiring anyone who did not have a seminary degree," was Cliff's curt reply to my request. This was one of those moments when you feel God speaking directly to you, giving you specific instructions. I knew God had spoken to us through Cliff, so I went back to school. A bonding began between myself and this seasoned pastor that has impacted me for life.

Eighteen months later, sheepskin in hand, I rolled back into town. I was shocked by what I heard from Cliff: "Oh, no, you do not understand. We are looking for a minister of education. You have the wrong degree!"

I do not know how I came up with the words, but I said confidently, "Cliff, don't you think you could do this job if it were yours to do, even with only a degree in theology?"

"Well, certainly," he retorted.

"Then what makes you think I can't?" I challenged.

"I am beginning to think you can!"

155

In the next several hours, Cliff walked me through the building. He talked—I listened. It was as if he was trying to talk me into my dream job. At the end of the evening, after the Wednesday-night prayer meeting, we prayed together. I will never forget his prayer: "Father, how you have knitted our hearts together as were David and Jonathan's. . . ."

Indeed, the Father did knit our hearts together. It was just a matter of time before I was hired. Cliff was a strong leader and usually got his way. He served and taught me as a father would a son. He pushed me into every kind of difficult circumstance that a minister experiences, like visiting terminally ill patients and conducting funerals of stillborn babies. He had me to do the Lord's Supper and baptisms, usually with no warning. He exposed me to deacons' meetings and let me in on his uncanny political savvy.

Trying Something New

I had not been here six months before the church struggled with its first "multi-congregational" decision: whether or not to start an additional Sunday-morning worship service at 8:30 A.M.

We had all the usual questions. Would people attend church at 8:30 in the morning? Would it divide the fellowship? Would the staff be able to hold up? Finally, we decided to take the plunge. Total attendance jumped 15 percent overnight.

The church had bumped up against that 80-percent capacity mark for years, and when we broke through, we never looked back. There has been some question about the wisdom of starting some of our services, but not about this one. That is why I am such a cheerleader for every church starting an early Sunday service. Even if you do not buy into the whole multi-congregational approach, this one step will help you greatly.

In retrospect, a couple of things we did seem very smart. For one thing, although the church had talked about this for several years, Cliff was a leader who had the good sense not to move too fast. If you are turning a ship, you need room to maneuver and time to check the waters. Otherwise, you might capsize the boat.

Another smart decision was having Cliff preach at this service. There *are* a finite number of times one pastor can preach in a weekend, but three is not too many. We also had the choir sing in the early service. (They stayed for Sunday school, sang again in the first part of the late service, and then slipped out inconspicuously.) I think having the choir there was fairly important in making the service a success. It legitimatized the service in many people's minds. More importantly, "forcing" this significant group of church leaders to attend the early service helped to create the critical mass. Elmer Towns places this number at 125.[1] This is about right, I think. I have been to churches that had only 35 people in the early service and it just did not feel like church. The desired number may be relative to the total size of the membership. For us, 125 was close to half. In fact, before we started the Saturday-night service, the 8:30 A.M. service on Sunday was fuller than the later one.

One other thing we did was give assurance to people that they would still see their friends during Sunday school and on Sunday night, when the whole fellowship would be together. This was one other side benefit of the second Sunday-morning service: a nice, full, robust Sunday-night experience.

The church rocked along, averaging about 8 percent growth per year during these days. In January of 1987, Cliff resigned, ushering in the worst year of my life. Cliff had been a strong and able leader. We were not prepared for life without him.

The Year of the Great Church Fight

I did some first-class, Grade A, USDA Choice, *dumb* things the year after Cliff left. To this day I would argue I was not malicious, and not outrightly more selfish than anybody else, but I was tops in the Dumb Department.

My basic mistake was deciding to wear three hats. I applied to be pastor, tried to influence people about who could and could not be pastor, and was preaching every Sunday. The church would have let me do any *one* of these—my choice. But I tried all three, and even my dad was amazed I survived. Fortunately, this church has a history of being gracious to staff members.

My efforts to influence this decision-making process were not very subtle. They were not careful political maneuverings behind the scenes. Instead, I stood up at the business meeting and publicly opposed the pulpit committee and their nominee. Not smart. For good reason, I had deacons coming after me and saying, "I am coming after your job."

I would not bring up this personal matter, except that it affects to this day Calvary's choices in regard to the multi-congregational approach. I am not sure which is the bigger issue, my insecurity from those scars, or the cautiousness that some members still feel about my preaching.[2] I suspect that to some the multi-congregational approach is a good idea—if it did not include my preaching in the service they attend. You do not get over these things quickly.

Ironically, the other struggle we have had over the multi-congregational approach stems from the fact that Sam Shaw, our current pastor, is an exceptional preacher. I have told him many times, "You know, Sam, our trouble is that you are just too good a preacher. If you were not quite so good, almost anyone would satisfy our members. But, as it is, every sermon has to be a ten. If you would occasionally hit some pop flies, we could pull this off a lot better." (By the way, God further demonstrated his love toward us in that while the pulpit committee and I were still enemies, God sent Sam, whom we all love. Sam and I are the best of friends.)

In all seriousness, we have found this to be an extremely important point. For the multi-congregation church to work, there must be an adequate number of equally competent preaching pastors. I am campaigning hard for our next staff addition to be someone who can share the preaching responsibilities. A church built on a strong pulpit needs a strong team on the dugout bench. There must be depth and consistency on that bench. You do not have to hit home runs every time, but you better be able to get a hit every time you come to the plate.

Sam's preaching skills, leadership ability, and vision stepped up our annual rate of growth to about 15 percent. In the first three months he was here, he led the church to adopt a goal of a thousand in attendance in Bible study by the year 2000. This galvanized the church into unified action. Sam and I attended the Saddleback Church Growth Conference eighteen months after he came. It proved to be a great help and inspiration, and implementing and adapting much of this philosophy of ministry enabled the church to continue growing.

Saturday Night's All Right for Worship

A year after Sam came to Calvary, we voted to start the Saturday-night worship service and Bible study. The decision was made a full three months before it was implemented. Prior to that, we talked to several groups: deacons, Sunday-school teachers, and the long-range planning committee. A lot of preparation time is necessary, especially when you are putting together a fully graded Sunday school. As previously mentioned, starting another service is a piece of cake, but adding another Sunday school is a first-class hassle.

The idea for Saturday worship originally surfaced in a deacons' class on church growth. This is something we do from time to time, and we have found it to be of great benefit to the church. You must teach the theory to the leaders before you ask them to act on it. This is especially true in a congregationally governed church. I will never forget the day Red Dixon first brought this up, seemingly out of the blue. The question was raised as to how we could reach people we were not yet reaching. Red said, "I think we should start a Saturday-night service for those who cannot attend on Sundays." It was far easier to sell an idea that "good ole Red" had come up with than a wild scheme that I—this new, young pastor—had dreamed up. So "I think we should do what Red suggested" became our slogan.

After we decided to do the Saturday-night service, we heard about Norm Whan's *The Phone's for You* telemarketing guide. We decided to attempt to call all 27,000 homes in Las Cruces in preparation for the new service, which was to start on January 28. The mistake we made was deviating from the suggested plan by trying to make the calls in a two-week period of time, between Christmas and New Year's Day. This proved to be insane. I personally made 623 calls. Our college intern, Ken Woods, made over 1,200. It completely stressed out all of us, and we put more pressure on the church body than was desirable. It was a frustrating feeling—I knew the process was working, but we just did not leave ourselves enough time to get it done.

We did get 19,000 calls made. Of that number, 1,300 people agreed to be on the mailing list and 125 showed up for our first service. There was a residual effect that lasted for years. Another intangible benefit was the hands-on feeling for the community it gave us. One thing I learned was that in our area, being a Baptist is not an asset. I don't know how many people I heard say, "If you are a Baptist, count me out."

My evaluation of telemarketing? I hate it, but it works. Although direct mail works about as well and is much less trouble, it is a bit more expensive. Telemarketing also has the downside of negatively impacting those who are already against you, whereas people are not generally offended by unsolicited mail—they just throw it away. Do not let me discourage you. If you are excited about doing telemarketing, go for it. It will reap rewards. But it is like driving a twenty-year-old car. If you have to drive one, it will get you by. If you can ever step up to direct mail, it is much easier than telemarketing and equally effective.

Here's an anecdote about our telemarketing drive. One couple got married as a result of it. Elaine, one of the young women helping us make the calls asked, "What is your name and address?"

The man on the other end said, "My name is Joe. What is *your* name? Could we meet sometime?" One thing led to another.

Another thing helped jump-start the Saturday-night service. We had two significant groups move en masse: the young marrieds who hated getting their kids up early on Sunday, and the young singles who loved staying out late at night. These two groups formed the critical mass of the new congregation.

We employed a contemporary style of worship in this service, replacing the piano, organ, and choir with a synthesizer, drums, and vocal band. At various times we added electric guitar and bass guitar. All this appealed to the younger, less conservative crowd. Traditionalists were not going to attend on Saturday night anyway, so we did not have to worry about offending them. One night the worship service included a "rock the walls" Christian rock group. Although this did not go over too well, it is significant that we did not hear any complaints. I shudder to think what would have happened if we had tried that on Sunday morning. I do not think we have the luxury of making those kind of mistakes.

The new style of music also attracted a different group of outsiders, people we were not reaching before. It sounded right to them. If you are reaching the right people with contemporary music, they may not know the songs, but the general sound will make sense to them. Instrumentation is a major factor in this.

Try this little experiment: Keep pushing the seek button on your FM radio until you find a station that is not talk and does not include drums in the sound. Almost impossible! Even "easy listening" will often include drums. Yet most of our churches do not use percussion instruments. And we wonder why young people stay away. The music needs to be familiar to them. Sure, there is more at work here than music—there is a full dimension of spiritual warfare operating. But, since I would not attend a service with country music, I can only assume that a generation raised on synthesizers, electric guitars, and drums will not be attracted by choirs, organs, and pianos.

"Your Young Men Will See Visions"

The truth of those words from Acts 2:17 came through to me in three successive music "visions." The first was at a Petra concert. I like Petra, but I am not swept into orbit by their music. Instead, I watched as two thousand kids went nuts over those sounds.

I wondered, "What happens to these kids on Sunday mornings when we sing, 'bringing in the sheaves, bringing in the sheaves, we shall come rejoicing. . . .'?"

It is easy enough to find out—just look at them on Sunday morning. During the service, they pass notes, they talk, they punch each other, they laugh. They are not bad kids. They are not really being mischievous, just bored. This came home to me when I attended a Saturday-night–style service on a Sunday night. The youth paid attention. They clapped, they sang, they participated. They didn't talk, punch each other, pass notes, or laugh.

After that Petra concert, I thought, "There has got to be a way to provide something for these kids that makes sense to them. Sure, we cannot have Petra in every week, but. . . . ." Later I walked by the lobby bar in the motel where we were staying. There was a little band playing. A light went on in my brain and I said to myself, "Surely there is enough talent in our church to put together a little group like that." It also occurred to me that this is the sort of thing Wesley did to fuel the fires of revival.

The second act of my vision was more private. A friend, Debbie Franzoy, had loaned me an Integrity Hosanna tape. One night around midnight I put on some headphones and began to listen in the dark. I listened in solitude, but I was not alone. God visited me that night in a profound way. I listened and listened and listened with tears streaming down my face. I knew this was it. We could not do Petra, but we could do something like this. The next day I brought the idea to the staff. We have a saying among our staff: "You got an idea, you got a job," so they said, "That is a great idea, Josh, and we look forward to seeing you do it."

I grabbed some of the best musicians in the church and put together a vocal band. Although I had not led music in ten years, for a year and a half I played conductor. The church was becoming multi-congregational. We were now in three services and had two different kinds of music. We were ministering to different people through those different styles. *Both* are right.

The third musical vision was at an Amy Grant concert. I looked around at perhaps six thousand kids who were going absolutely bonkers and said to myself again, "We owe it to this generation to communicate the gospel in a way that musically connects." It was such a vivid confirmation that we were on course. If you have never been to a concert, this kind of language is foreign to you. It is a completely right-brained concept. Especially if you are male, you probably do not talk to your right brain often enough.

If you think music is "no big deal," it is probably because the music in the service you attend is acceptable to you. I have heard many say, "Music should not matter. The church is not in the entertainment business. People should just be attracted by the gospel." This is all well and good as long as you like the music. Put this the other way around. If music is not that important, why not play music *you* hate if it will keep our kids in church? Can't we ask our older adults to put up with sounds they do not like, instead of boring our young people? Often, when people fight for "just keeping it simple," they are really arguing for the way they like it.

This Land Is Your Land, This Land Is My Land

Once we got the Saturday-night service started, we thought it would buy us enough time to get another building constructed. We had a committee in place and functioning when some adjacent land became available—part of the original acreage sold back when this site was selected. We knew this was part of our future. We would have to delay building if we purchased the land, but we knew it was wise to do so. This twist of circumstances caused us to run out of space again before we could get new facilities built. We had to provide more space soon.

When we brought forward the plan to add 9:45 Sunday worship, the people took it in stride. They had almost become used to the idea of starting new services. The college group moved to the 9:45 service and Sunday school at

11:00, forming our critical mass. Because we were all well entrenched in the multi-service model, moving within this model was no strain.

However, when we sought to lead the church toward starting a fifth primary service and a second Sunday-evening service, it was a new ball game. People understood intuitively that this would mean that their pastor could not preach all the time.

I mentioned in chapter 2 that two things distinguish a multi-service church model from one that is multi-congregation. The former model has only one preaching pastor, but the latter has more than one. Also, a multi-service church has one believers' service, whereas a multi-congregation church has more than one.[3] Thus, although we risked dividing the core when we added a second Sunday-evening service, here began the shift to a true multi-congregational church.

To get past this barrier, we began educating people about the multi-congregational approach. It was for this reason that I wrote this book, which started out as a paper distributed to Calvary's leaders and later was circulated among the rank and file of the church. Everyone needed generous dosages of time and information to adjust to the idea.

I cannot overstate the tension of breaking into this new paradigm. There were several failed experiments. We started two evening worship services, only to cancel one later. We started a 12:15 service, which did not work either. We tried everything: two different preaching pastors, three different preaching approaches, two different musical styles, three different worship leaders. I begged and pleaded and went into the highways and byways, and people still would not come. We failed to heed the principles that people follow trusted leaders and move as a group. We never got a group to help us with the 12:15 service. Nine months later, it was history.

Overcrowding at the 9:45 service at Calvary led to our next idea: try an off-campus service at 9:30. We considered a couple of places that would be suitable and settled on a local theater. This time we remembered that people follow leaders and move in groups, so Sam (the senior pastor) "moved" to become leader of that congregation, while another man and myself shared the preaching at the central location. We were afraid that due to Sam's popularity, creating a service at the theater would kill the 9:45 service here, but we hoped we would end up with a viable congregation in both locations. All our hopes were realized. Our fears never came to pass. The original group divided about evenly, and we now have a group of over a hundred in the satellite congregation, with room to grow in both places. The system seems to be working. Although we do not know if the satellite congregation will eventually become an independent church or continue in a satellite relationship indefinitely, either way is a winning proposition.

Starting the satellite has hurt our on-campus Sunday-school attendance in the short run. Many who were previously going to Sunday school are now helping with the satellite instead. We are starting home groups to support the satellite, but these will not be counted in our Sunday-school attendance. Doing a project like this requires a kingdom mentality that looks beyond the raw statistics.

Every location in which we can offer the gospel will reach some people that other sites will not. It is not that one location is better than another; each can target a different group. There is not one location that could reach everyone, even if space were not a problem. People who are attracted by the stability and convenience of a traditional building will not be moved by a church in the theater. Others like a relaxed, informal atmosphere and would be more comfortable in a theater than in a church. One thing a church may have to give up with an off-campus location is the convenience of being able to provide a fully graded Sunday school for the new congregation.

The satellite service gave us the opportunity to begin an 8:30 Sunday school. Our 8:30 worship service has always been more popular than the 11:00 service. I learned from this that people in our area would rather come early and leave early—get church "out of the way." I have always felt that if we could get an 8:30 Sunday school going, it would be more popular than the one at 11:00. We could not experiment with this before the satellite was created, because we could not afford to have people moving from the 8:30 and 11:00 services to the one at 9:45. Now that the 9:45 service has some extra seats, we can move in this direction.

A New Building and a Master Plan

Plans are underway for a larger building, which, for a while, will eliminate the *necessity* of adding more services. (People generally don't do what they don't have to.) We are holding our breath to see what happens when we move into the new facilities. If they fill up rather quickly, we will probably implement the next stages of multi-congregational development, but we do not know if we will cancel any services when the new building is available.

In the meantime, we are working through the process of getting widespread ownership of the master plan (similar to appendix B). The culmination of distributing this proposal will be the formal adoption of a plan that will list the services we hope to have in place in the future, as well as what will be needed to accomplish this—building size, number of staff, capital fund raising, advertising budget, and so on. Once the plan is in place, we will be able to chart a smooth course toward aggressive growth without worrying too much about unpleasant surprises.

As of now, our schedule is as follows, although we will continue to make adjustments as needed:

Saturday	6:00 P.M.	Contemporary Worship
	7:15 P.M.	Bible Study (Sunday School)
Sunday	7:15 A.M.	Early-Bird Sunday School (one class only)
	8:30 A.M.	Traditional Worship Sunday School
	9:30 A.M.	Satellite Service (at Video 4 Theater)
	9:45 A.M.	Contemporary Worship (senior pastor does not preach) Sunday School
	11:00 A.M.	Traditional Worship Sunday School
	5:00 P.M.	Discipleship Training
	6:00 P.M.	Believers' Worship

Epilogue

Let me leave every church with a challenge to do just one thing: *Start one more service*. Do it as I described in chapter 8, and punch it with all the advertising you can afford.

One nice thing about the multi-congregation church is that it lends itself to experimentation. I do not know how many services a particular church can handle. For us, I think it is something more than seven. But you do not need that many services to reap the benefits of the multi-congregational model. Just start one more. When you see that one service can double your efficiency, you may decide to go further.

On July 15, 1982, Donald Bennett realized his lifelong dream of standing on the summit of Mount Rainier. It took him five days, but he was the first amputee to scale the 14,410-foot mountain. In fact, he really did it twice. A year earlier, a howling windstorm had kept him a few hundred feet from the crest. When asked how he did it, Bennett replied, "One hop at a time." That is how you become a multi-congregation church: one hop at a time. By the way, Don Bennett also revealed another secret. On one difficult section, his daughter stayed by his side and for four hours whispered in his ear, "You can do it, Dad. You are the best dad in the world. You can do it." I want to say to you: "You can do it. God is on your side."[1]

Who knows? You may fall in love with the multi-congregational approach, as I have. I love its vision—its diversity, its potential, its innovative freshness. I love its theory and I love its practice. (I even thrill to its hassle.)

I dream of giving my two boys a rich legacy, a generation of churches that is positioned to carry out the Great Commission as God intended.

Want to come along?

Appendix A

A Changing Population

Sometimes having a bias will actually motivate you to find information to back up a pet theory. So it is with the graphs you are about to see. I did not stumble on this data accidentally. I started by assuming that the traditional church is less effective in fulfilling the Great Commission than it once was.

All statistics come from the *1992 World Almanac*,[1] the *1992 Southern Baptist Handbook*,[2] and the U.S. Census Bureau.

The last graph may need a little explaining. The formulas are a bit complex, but it is the most persuasive graph to me. It demonstrates visually the rising cost of buildings per new member, adjusted for per capita giving, compared with the simultaneous decrease in number of new members.

These graphs, of course, do not prove anything. They do, I think, give plausible reason why the multi-congregation church is needed today where it may not have been as important in recent years. We have never had five billion people with an address on planet earth. I hope these graphs encourage further study, contemplation, and analysis.

To justify my proposals for an alternative approach to "doing church," I wanted some statistics to verify the truth of what I suspected. In effect, I needed conclusive answers to two related sets of questions. First, was there indeed a decrease in percentage of church attenders in the general population? Second, was there a concurrent change in population demographics that might partially explain this decline? If, as I suspected, our society had become increasingly urbanized and its population more densely packed, the law of supply and demand would increase the per capita cost of adding new members to the point where a church would stifle its own growth potential and dampen the enthusiasm of its existing members. This would be expected to show up as *both* a decline in the percentage of churched members in the population and also as giving levels that did not keep up with the dramatic rise in building costs.

Although the following graphs appear to prove that the church has a problem, they do not necessarily suggest that the multi-congregational approach is the only answer. But, if the traditional church is not working as it should in a modern society, the real question remains: How can we improve on its delivery system?

U.S. Urban and Rural Population
(in millions)

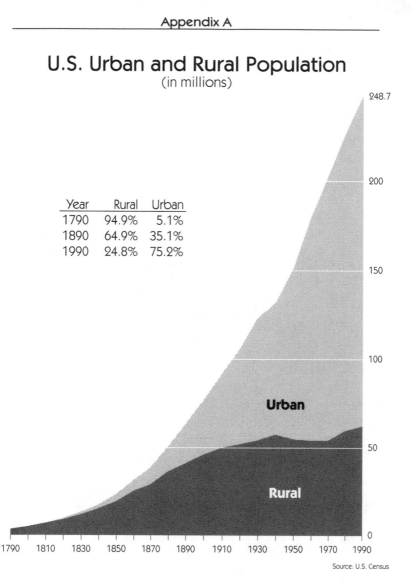

Year	Rural	Urban
1790	94.9%	5.1%
1890	64.9%	35.1%
1990	24.8%	75.2%

Source: U.S. Census

The population of the United States has grown sharply. While rural population has leveled off, urban population has skyrocketed.

173

Churched Population 1960–90
(in millions)

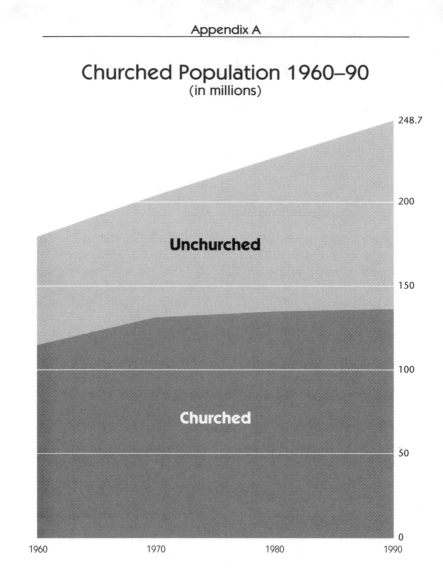

Church growth has been slow compared to population growth. In 1960, 64% of the population was on a church roster. In 1980, less than 60% of the population was on a church roster.

Dollars Spent on Buildings Per New Member 1940–90
(Southern Baptists, in thousand dollars)

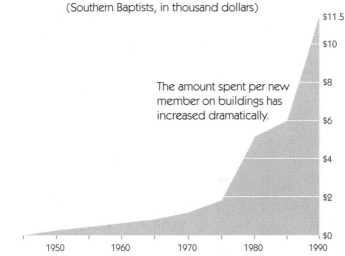

The amount spent per new member on buildings has increased dramatically.

Per Capita Giving 1940–90
(Southern Baptist churches)

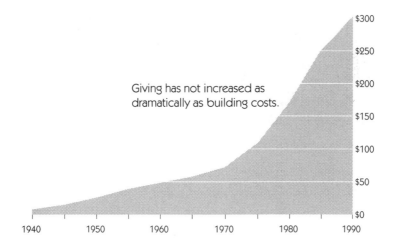

Giving has not increased as dramatically as building costs.

Southern Baptist Membership Growth
(in millions)

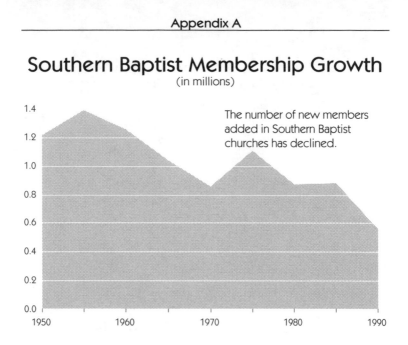

The number of new members added in Southern Baptist churches has declined.

Southern Baptist Growth in Assets
(in billions)

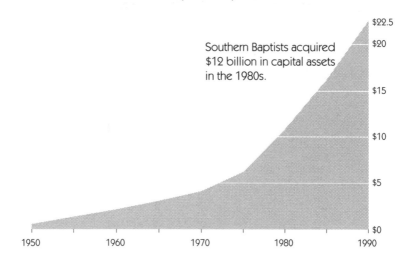

Southern Baptists acquired $12 billion in capital assets in the 1980s.

Members Added & Expenses Rise
(expenses in thousand dollars)

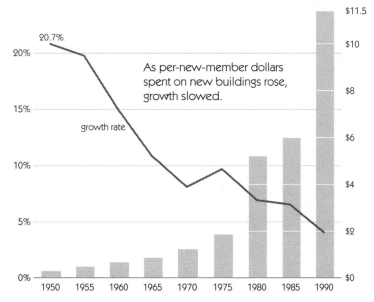

20.7%

As per-new-member dollars
spent on new buildings rose,
growth slowed.

growth rate

Appendix B

A Sample Master Plan

Following is a sample master plan for a church. It provides an outline of the kind of broad planning I think is important to the ongoing health of the church. It ensures that we have adequate staff and other resources to serve our various congregations and encourages growth. The heart and soul of the plan is the page with all the numbers. This page specifies the number of services and all the related factors. We intend for this plan to be a living document that will be updated each year. One of its many advantages is that it will allow us to spread out our fund-raising efforts and capital expenditures over an extended period of time. We hope there will be no unpleasant surprises.

Master Plan

Bright Star Community Church

Enjoying God and Sharing the Joy!

2000 by 2000

Purpose

The purpose of Bright Star Community Church is to glorify God by making disciples of Jesus Christ. A disciple is one who enjoys God and is working together with fellow disciples to share the joy.

Goal

The goal of Bright Star Community Church is to have 2000 in small Bible study groups by the year 2000. This may include on-site Sunday school type groups as well as off campus groups.

Philosophy of Ministry

Principle #1 Quality is more important than quantity. God has called us to make disciples, not converts. The result of our ministry should be praying, holy, joyful, committed, loving, spirit-filled Christians.

Principle #2 Principle #1 is just barely true. That is, quantity is also important. The work of our ministry should result in measurable, "graphable" church growth.

Principle #3 The ministry belongs to the laymen. The role of laymen is not to help the staff with their ministry. Rather, the role of staff is to equip the saints in their ministry. Ownership of ministry is the key to long-term motivation and effectiveness.

Principle #4 Disciples are made in small groups. Most of the ministry—teaching one another, admonishing one another, encouraging one another, loving one another, serving one another, etc.—happens in small groups. We measure our success, therefore, by attendance in small groups.

Principle #5 The goal of every small group should be to double every two years or less. By this we mean that each group should give birth to a new group every two years.

Principle #6 Groups can double every two years or less by inviting every member and every prospect to every fellowship every month. Most people who are opposed to the gospel are not opposed to ice cream. Fellowships are the front door to our groups.

Principle #7 Every member is encouraged and expected to use their gifts to grow their group.

Principle #8 The chief end of man is to enjoy God and glorify Him forever. All of our service should flow out of a love relationship with God.

Principle #9 God is at work in the world around us. It is better to discover what God is doing and join Him in it than to dream up something good to do for God. We discover what God is doing by cultivating a love relationship with Him.

Approach

We believe the multi-congregation approach is the most efficient and effective way to approach ministry. We believe this is what God has called this congregation to.

The multi-congregation church is described in the book entitled *Let it Grow*, and details of the approach can be obtained there. However, the multi-congregation approach as a congregation can be summarized as a congregation that sees herself as a group of interrelated groups with several preaching pastors and numerous meeting times for both small groups and worship service. The church will not purchase facilities large enough for the entire congregation to meet in, although they may rent such facilities on an occasional basis.

There are two primary advantages of the multi-congregation approach. The first is the tremendous savings on capital resources. This savings has the advantage of reducing the pressure on a congregation often associated with building programs and fund raising drives. It also frees money to be spent on advertising, missions and equippers for ministry.

The second advantage of the multi-congregation approach is the diversity of programming it enables us to offer to people. People are not all alike. By offering different approaches in terms of worship style, preaching approach and small group meetings we will be more effective in reaching a larger number of people.

Why a Plan?

The purpose of this plan is not to make decisions today that can be made better with the advantage of up-to-date information. Many decisions, such as what staff positions to fill, whether to hire full time or part time staff and what times to add services can be better answered as the decision approaches. We mean for this plan to be as flexible and open to change as possible. It is to be a living document, subject to review each year.

The purpose of this plan is to provide one possible avenue of growth. If other avenues of growth become available, and it seems prudent at the time to take these, then we should do so. What a plan does for us is to foresee when new buildings will need to be built, when new staff will need to be called and when new services will need to be started. This way, we can be confident that we will not run out of space at a time when we have no money to build and no money to hire additional staff to help with additional services. Stress points can be spotted well ahead of time and corrected on paper before they become a reality.

If the actual growth rate is higher or lower than the projection here, it will not substantially alter the nature of the plan. It may be that we will be at the 1997 level in 1998 or 1996. But, the things that must happen (number of services, number of staff and size of buildings) will all need to take place at the same time.

Assumptions

Assumption #1 By adopting the multiple congregation model, we will be able to reach an average attendance of 2000 in Bible study by the year 2000. This will be made possible by (1) providing ample staff, (2) spending significant dollars on advertising, (3) controlling costs of buildings and the negative impact of fund-raising campaigns, (4) having a varied menu that offers something for a broad range of people. Growth will need to average 17% per year in order to reach this goal.

Assumption #2 The church will be willing to adopt the multi-congregation approach. Following this plan we will be building larger buildings (a multi-purpose building in 1991, education space in 1994, and a worship center in 1998, additional education space in 2002) as well as add additional services. Following this plan we will have seven seeker's services, six Bible study times, three believer's services, and four people (in addition to the pastor) who will be sharing the preaching responsibility.

Assumption #3 When an auditorium or education building is 80% full it will begin to negatively affect the growth potential of the church. Because it is impossible to keep all services even, we can assume that some services will be at or past the 80% mark. When the overall building (capacity times the number of times it is used divided by the number in attendance) is at 60% there will be stresses in the program that are negatively affecting the growth of the church. Therefore, it is in the best interest of the church to keep overall capacity less than 60%.

Assumption #4 It is not wise to ask a preaching pastor to preach more than 4 times per week. If this pastor is devoting part time to preaching and part time to other program responsibility (i.e. singles, etc.) then he should not preach more than 2 times per week. The plan carefully balances the addition of new services with the calling of additional staff members who can share the preaching responsibility. Similarly, some of the other program staff need to be able to assist in music in some of the services. It is also assumed that competent preachers who will also take on other responsibilities can be found. The specific job titles are suggestive. Needs will be analyzed as the time arises. The key aspect of the plan is that the number of staff keep pace with the growth of the church.

Assumption #5 We assume that we can spend with great profit up to 5% of our budget on advertising. However, it is assumed that this will have a gradually declining effectiveness as the dollar amount grows higher. Therefore, the percentage rises to 5% then declines slightly, while the dollar amount continues to rise.

Assumption #6 The larger the church the more efficient the staff to attendance ratio can be. There is a gradual spreading of this ratio from 1:85 in 1990 to 1:154 in 2000. This number should in no case exceed 1:250. Note that this ratio is based on Sunday school attendance, not worship attendance.

Assumption #7 It is assumed that giving will maintain a ratio of $1000 per year per person who attends Sunday school. This has been our consistent pattern for many years. This plan is not adjusted for inflation because it was felt that 1991 dollars would be more meaningful numbers.

Assumption #8 Capital expenses raised in any one year should not exceed 15% of the budget except in years that a building is completed. It is assumed that the excitement of seeing an actual project completed will generate enough enthusiasm to make it possible to raise this kind of money. If we get past the completion of the current multi-purpose building, we will never have large capital fund-raising efforts of this magnitude again.

Assumption #9 Bright Star Community Church wants to be obedient to the Great Commission and believes that obedience to the Great Commission includes numerical growth as well as internal, spiritual growth.

Assumption #10 God is willing to bless the progress of His church. We must depend on Him drawing people unto Himself. Without Him we can do nothing. In all our ways we acknowledge Him. We believe God is willing and able to draw people unto Himself as we cooperate with Him as ministers—as if we were His ambassadors.

Strategies

In order to accomplish the goal of 2000 by 2000, it will be necessary for us to do seven things:

- attract visitors
- encourage visitors to return
- encourage people to join
- assimilate new members
- care for the people of God
- develop leadership
- organize the work of God

Each of these will need to be monitored independently to assure balanced, consistent growth. Each one affects the others.

This section will discuss briefly plans and strategies to accomplish each of these.

How to Attract Visitors

Unless visitors visit, the church cannot grow. Goals can be set, buildings constructed, programs put into place and services planned, but it is all for nothing if we do not have new people visiting our services.

The bread and butter of our strategy for attracting new visitors is a word of mouth strategy. We fully expect that the bulk of our visitors will come from the personal invitation of members and attenders. We will attempt to capitalize on this by making our seeker's services visitor friendly. We will evaluate these services through the eyes of visitors. Members and regular attenders should feel this is a safe place to bring friends. They will not be embarrassed. Topics for sermons will be selected in part on the basis of their attractiveness to outsiders. The music should make sense to outsiders. They may not know the songs, but it should sound right to them. Words and phases that are difficult for the uninitiated to understand will be avoided. The idea of communicating the gospel in a way that makes sense to outsiders is as old as the Apostle Paul, who said, "I have become all things to all men so that by all possible means I might save some." We will never change the age-old message, but we will seek to communicate it in a way that the uninitiated can hear. A variety of approaches in worship services will help to reach even more people. Some services will be more traditional, others more contemporary, while still others may have a different format altogether.

In addition to word of mouth advertising, media advertising will be utilized. We believe that up to 5% of our budget can be used profitably on advertising. Media advertising has two advantages. First, it reinforces the word of mouth advertising done by our members and regular attenders by making the church a familiar name to outsiders. Second, it allows us to penetrate pools of people that have no relational contact with members of Bright Star Community. These people, once attracted, can help us through their word of mouth testimony.

Several times a year we will have special events designed especially to be attractive to outsiders. For example, Easter will be a big celebration each year. On these days we expect to spike attendance to new levels. Attendance is expected to drop after the big event, but to a higher level than it was previously.

How to Encourage Visitors to Return

If a visitor attends a second time the chances of him coming a third and a fourth rise sharply. Our opportunity to make a disciple out of this individual and utilize their service in helping others is greatly increased.

The most important way to attract visitors to come back is to provide a quality experience for them when they are here. Music shall be done in a way that is tasteful, relevant and demonstrates excellence. Sermons will be delivered in such a way as to be interesting, clear, relevant and biblical. Greeters will be utilized to insure that a friendly atmosphere is communicated.

After visitors leave, an overlapping strategy of contact shall be maintained. A pastoral letter will be sent. One or more phone calls will be made. They will receive the newsletter for several months after they visit. Sunday school classes and small groups will contact them. Staff will make contacts as time allows.

Principles considered in contacting visitors are:

The more personal the contact, the more effective. Hand written notes are better than computer merged letters. An invitation to a home is more effective than an invitation to another church event. We have found that if a visitor receives and accepts an invitation to an individual's home fellowship, chances are 90% or better that they will join.

The more immediate the contact the more effective. Contacts made on Sunday afternoon or Monday evening are more effective than contacts made a week or more after the visitor visits.

The more contacts the better. It would be advantageous for each visitor to receive seven contacts the first week after their visit. Several invitations to different groups' activities have a better chance of reaching the person than only one contact.

How to Encourage People to Join

People who visit the church are from several distinct groups. On one end of the spectrum are those who are long time Christians and are already living the disciple's life. On the other end are seekers who are exploring the Christian faith for the first time.

Surprisingly, the method of getting either group to come to church membership is similar: get them to know some people in the church. When people know seven friends in the church, you will not keep them away. People find it easier to embrace the faith of their friends. They like to become Christians without crossing cultural, language, ethnic, or social barriers.

Obviously, the seeker must learn much to become a disciple. He must learn much to become a Christian. He must repent of his sin, place his faith in Christ, and surrender to Christ as Lord. Worship services will be planned with this in mind. The gospel will be presented in most services, with an opportunity to respond. But getting him acquainted with several friends in the church is as important to him as becoming a Christian and a disciple as is educational content.

Names of visitors will be assigned to individuals gifted in this ministry who will attempt to befriend them and introduce them to others in various groups in the church. An attempt will be made to match people according to age, sex, and marital status.

How to Assimilate New Members

Assimilation of new members begins before they join. If visitors have been treated properly from the time they fill out a card they should be well on their way to being assimilated into the life of the body by the time they join.

When they join they will be personally counseled by a trained counselor. He will verify their understanding and experience of salvation. Their baptism will be discussed. What it means to be a member of the church will be discussed. They will be enrolled in a small group. It should be impossible to be a member of the church and not be enrolled in a small group. Small groups are the lifeblood of the assimilation process. Every small group should have someone in charge of inreach, outreach and monthly fellowships. Every member and every visitor should be invited to every fellowship every month. If this is done, the group will double every two years or less.

CareGivers will also be assigned to all new members. They will contact them on a monthly basis and see that they are progressing into several meaningful friendships and growing in grace and knowledge.

Classes will be offered on a regular basis that will help new members and new believers obtain the information they need to progress in their personal discipleship journey.

How to Care for the People of God

Jesus taught that the church would be known by its love. The desire of this church is to be one that is marked by a profound and practical love for each other. Every member, regardless of spiritual maturity, length of membership, age, or attendance habits should be loved by the body. In order for this to happen an intentional pastoral care system must be maintained. The heart of the Pastoral Care System is the deacon-led CareGiver System. The work of the CareGiver can be summarized as follows:

C Contacts each person at least once a month.
A Available always, especially in emergencies.
R Remember in prayer daily.
E Example: CareGivers should live the kind of life where they would say, "Follow me as I follow Christ."

CareGivers are laymen with gifts such as mercy and encouragement that allow them to minister effectively to a group of five to ten individuals.

The deacons shall be involved as "Partners" in the CareGiving ministry. Each staff member will be assigned several deacons who will be assigned several CareGivers to provide care for, as described above. A big part of the function of the staff will be to make the individual CareGiver on the front line effective in his ministry. Staff will also model loving care for individuals, but the main part of the caring will take place on an individual basis between CareGiver and member.

How to Develop Leadership

Leadership is essential to any growing movement. Growing churches demand growing leaders. Every leader will be expected to be in an ongoing, lifelong learning system. The fields are white unto harvest. The laborers are few.

The best leadership development is leadership by example. Every worker, regardless of their area of ministry, should have an apprentice who is being trained to take their place. Every teacher should be training another to teach, so that when the need arises to lead another group a trained, experienced leader is available.

In addition to this personal approach, regular classes will be offered in Discipleship Training Program in leadership skill development. Sermons in the believer's services will be pitched to leaders.

A consistent ratio of staff to attendance will be needed in order to equip leaders. A major part of every staff member's job will be leadership development. The role of staff members is not so much doing ministry as it is equipping the saints to do the work of the ministry.

How to Organize the Work of God

Organization of the church should be maintained to maximize ministry and minimize maintenance. We need enough people to give adequate representation in decision making, but not so many that the system is bogged down. We do not want to unnecessarily tie up people's time so that they cannot give themselves to ministry.

The organization of the church should optimize communication. We believe in keeping as much information as possible as open to as many people as possible.

The organization will need to be reevaluated and changed periodically. Every time an organization grows 40% it will require a complete change in organization.

The organization should provide for a system of checks and balances. If there were a thief in the house, the system should catch the thief.

The organization should breed confidence in all members that decisions are being made responsibly, plans are being carried out in a prudent manner, and finances are carefully accounted for.

What Is a Disciple?

Jesus told us to make disciples, not converts. A disciple is one who is a fully devoted follower of Christ who displays a level of maturity and is growing in his faith. The acrostic D.I.S.C.I.P.L.E. will aid our memory in understanding the kind of person we are trying to produce.

D Disciplined in his daily devotional life.

I Involved in a small group. Disciples are not lone rangers, they are involved in the life of a group.

S Spirit-filled. A disciple knows what it is to live out the Spirit-filled life on a day-to-day basis.

C Concerned for others. The me-centeredness has been broken in a true disciple of Christ.

I Involved in ministry in the area of his giftedness.

P Prayerful always.

L Learner. The Greek word for disciple means learner or student. A disciple is pursuing the moving goal of personal godliness.

E Enjoys God. The Christian life is one of joy. Because disciples enjoy God, they are eager to share the joy with others.

How to Grow a Group

The basic engine for the growth of the church—both numerical growth and spiritual growth—is the small group. We believe that a small group, properly organized, can double every two years or less. The detail of this plan is in the book *You Can*

Appendix B

GOALS & PROJECTIONS:	1986	1987	1988	1989	1990	1991
SS Attendance	270	276	319	367	425	490
Worship Attendance	400	450	500	525	600	686
Believer's Service	175	200	200	250	300	343
% Growth, SS		2%	16%	15%	16%	15%
% Growth, Worship		13%	11%	5%	14%	14%
Budget (in $1,000)	260	280	319	367	425	480
SCHEDULE AND POTENTIAL ATTENDANCE						
Seeker's Service (Potential)	500	500	500	750	1000	1250
Seeker's Service Schedule				Sat	Sat	Sat
	8:30	8:30	8:30	8:30	8:30	8:30
					9:45	9:45
	11:00	11:00	11:00	11:00	11:00	11:00
						12:15
SS (Potential)	300	300	300	600	900	900
SS Schedule				Sat	Sat	Sat
	9:45	9:45	9:45	9:45	9:45	9:45
					11:00	11:00
Believer's Service (Potential)	250	250	250	250	250	500
Believer's Service Schedule	6:00	6:00	6:00	6:00	6:00	5:00
						6:15
SPACE AVAILABLE & FUNDRAISING						
Auditorium 80% full	250	250	250	250	250	250
SS 80% Full	300	300	300	300	300	300
Capital Fund Raising			60,000	75,000	75,000	200,000
Capitol as a % of Budget			19%	20%	18%	42%35%
Construction Project			Nehemiah	Land	Land	Start Multi
Extra SS Space	24	-19	233	475	410	635
Percent Full, SS	90%	92%	106%	61%	47%	54%
Extra Worship Space	100	50	0	225	400	564
Percent Full, Worship	80%	90%	100%	70%	60%	55%
Extra Believer's Seats	75	50	50	0	-50	157
% Believer's Service	70%	80%	80%	100%	120%	69%
ADVERTISING						
Advertising %				1%	2%	3%
Advertising Budget				$3,670	$8,500	$14,400
STAFF						
Staff (number)	4	4	4	4	5	5
Ratio	68	69	80	92	85	98
Preaching Pastors (number)	1	1	1	1	1	1.5
Services per pastor	3.0	3.0	3.0	4.0	5.0	4.7
Possible positions	Pastor	Pastor	Pastor	Pastor	Pastor	Pastor
	Music	Music	Music	Music	Music	Music
	Ed.	Ed.	Ed.	Ed.	Ed.	Ed.*
	Youth	Youth	Youth	Youth	Youth	Youth
					Child/Pre	Child/Pre

*Shares preaching part time
Note: Staff titles are meant to be examples. Actual need will be assessed as they arise.

1992	1993	1994	1995	1996	1997	1998	1999	2000
565	655	765	900	1050	1225	1450	1700	2000
791	917	1071	1260	1470	1715	2030	2380	2800
396	458	536	630	735	858	1015	1190	1400
15%	16%	17%	18%	17%	17%	18%	17%	18%
15%	16%	17%	18%	17%	17%	18%	17%	18%
565	655	765	900	1,050	1,225	1,450	1,700	2,000
2000	2400	2400	2400	2400	2400	3000	3600	4200
Sat	Sat	Sat	Sat	Sat	Sat	Sat	Sat	Sat
8:30	8:30	8:30	8:30	8:30	8:30	8:30	8:30	8:30
9:45	9:45	9:45	9:45	9:45	9:45	9:45	9:45	9:45
11:00	11:00	11:00	11:00	11:00	11:00	11:00	11:00	11:00
						12:15	12:15	12:15
							Sat #2	Sat #2
								Friday
1200	1350	1350	1350	1500	1800	2400	2800	3200
Sat	Sat	Sat	Sat	Sat	Sat	Sat	Sat	Sat
						8:30	8:30	8:30
9:45	9:45	9:45	9:45	9:45	9:45	9:45	9:45	9:45
11:00	11:00	11:00	11:00	11:00	11:00	11:00	11:00	11:00
500	600	1200	1200	1200	1200	1800	1800	1800
6:00	6:00	5:00	5:00	5:00	5:00	5:00	5:00	5:00
		6:30	6:30	6:30	6:30	6:30	6:30	6:30
						Wed	Wed	Wed
500	600	600	600	600	600	600	600	600
400	450	450	450	500	600	600	700	800
200,000	200,000	100,000	100,000	200,000	200,000	200,000	200,000	200,000
35%	31%	13%	11%	19%	16%	14%	12%	10%
				Start Education	Complete Education			
635	695	585	450	450	575	950	1100	1200
47%	49%	57%	67%	70%	68%	60%	61%	63%
1209	1483	1329	1140	930	685	970	1220	1400
40%	38%	45%	53%	61%	71%	68%	66%	67%
104.5	141.5	664.5	570	465	342.5	785	610	400
79%	76%	45%	53%	61%	71%	56%	66%	78%
4%	5%	5%	5%	5%	4.5%	4%	3.5%	3.5%
$22,600	$32,750	$38,250	$45,000	$52,500	$55,125	$58,000	$59,500	$70,000
5.5	6	7	8	9	10	11	12	13
103	109	109	113	117	123	132	142	154
2	2	2	2	2	2	2.5	2.5	3
2.5	2.5	3.0	3.0	3.0	3.0	3.2	3.6	3.3
Pastor	Pastor	Pastor	Pastor	Pastor	Pastor	Pastor	Pastor	Pastor
Music	Music	Music	Music	Music	Music	Music	Music	Music
Ed.*	Ed.*	Ed.*	Ed.*	Ed.*	Ed.*	Ed.*	Ed.*	Ed.*
Youth	Youth	Youth	Youth	Youth	Youth	Youth	Youth	Youth
Child/Pre	Child/Pre	Child/Pre	Child/Pre	Children	Children	Children	Children	Children
Singles*	Singles*	Singles*	Singles*	Singles*	Singles*	Singles*	Singles*	Singles*
		College	College	College	College	College	College	College
			Sr. Adult	Sr. Adult	Sr. Adult	Sr. Adult	Sr. Adult	Sr. Adult
				Preschool	Preschool	Preschool	Preschool	Preschool
					Admin	Admin	Admin	Admin
						Yng Adult	Yng Adult	Yng Adult
							Evangelism*	Evangelism*
								Prayer*

Double Your Class in Two Years or Less by Josh Hunt. To summarize, a group can double every two years or less if . . .

- A teacher presents a quality lesson each week that is biblical, practical, interesting and clear.
- A fellowship leader plans a fellowship each month that is fun to the group.
- An outreach leader invites every prospect to every fellowship every month.
- An inreach leader contacts absentees, invites every member to every fellowship every month and cares for the needs of the group.
- Someone is responsible for hospitality and will give Friday nights to Jesus hosting members and prospects for fellowships in their home.
- A prayer coordinator prays for the needs of the group.
- A class president coordinates the work of the group.
- The group is willing to give birth to a new group as they pass 15 in attendance.

You can double your group in two years or less by inviting every member and every prospect to every fellowship every month.

— Josh Hunt

Endnotes

Chapter 1: A Tale of an American Church

1. I borrow the terminology from Bill Hybels, the senior pastor at Willow Creek (Illinois) Community Church.

2. George Barna, *The Frog in the Kettle* (Ventura, Calif.: Regal Books, 1990), p. 137.

3. Ibid., p. 135.

4. I am using the terminology adopted from Lyle Schaller and widely used in church-growth literature to describe those who have been members of the church a long time and those who have come more recently.

Chapter 2: Three Kinds of Churches

1. John R. W. Stott, *The Spirit, the Church, and the World* (Downer's Grove, Ill.: InterVarsity Press, 1990), p. 236.

2. Ibid., p. 324.

3. Joel Arthur Barker, *Future Edge* (New York: William Morrow, 1992), p. 32.

4. John Vaughan, "Characteristics of Growing Churches," *Growing Churches,* January, February, March, 1991, p. 16.

5. Timm Boyle, Willow Creek, October 1990, p. 7.

6. Benno Schmidt, Jr., *Wall Street Journal,* quoted in Chuck Swindoll, *Rise and Shine* (Portland, Ore.: Multnomah, 1989), p. 111.

7. I might point out that I am using a different definition than that used by Peter Wagner and others to describe an Anglo church that has other ethnic congregations meeting in the same facilities. Although that would fit my definition of multi-congregational, my example of a multi-congregation church that is mono-cultural seems outside the bounds of his thinking in *Church Planting for a Greater Harvest* (Ventura, Calif.: Regal, 1990), pp. 67ff.

8. Peter Senge, *The Fifth Discipline* (New York: Doubleday, 1990).

9. Roland Allen, *The Spontaneous Expansion of the Church and the Causes Which Hinder It* (Grand Rapids: Eerdmans, 1962), p. 6.

10. Henry Blackaby, from the tape series, *"Experiencing God."*

Chapter 3: Is the Everyday Church Biblical?

1. Although not as clearly as some would have us believe. Justin (*Anti-Nicene Fathers,* vol. 1, p. 186), for example, says, "Sunday is the day on which we all hold our common assembly." But, in the writing called, "The Teaching of the Apostles" (*Anti-Nicene Fathers,* vol. 8, p. 668), we read, "The apostles further appointed: on the first day of the week let there be service, and reading of the Holy Scriptures." However, this same writing goes on to say, "The Apostles further appointed: on the fourth day of the week let there be a service, because on that day our Lord made the disclosure to them about the trial. . . . The Apostles further appointed: on the eve of the Sabbath, at the ninth hour, let there be a service: because that which had been spoken on the fourth day of the week about the suffering of the Saviour was brought to pass. . . ." They also appointed several yearly celebrations as well as these prescribed weekly meetings. I guess you could describe the church at this point as semi-everyday. Those who support Sunday-only worship tend to cite only those passages from the Fathers that support their position.

2. John Scott, Sr., *The Lord's Day* (Nashville: Broadman, 1986), p. 114.

3. D. K. Lowery, *Evangelical Dictionary of Theology,* Walter Elwell, ed. (Grand Rapids: Baker, 1984), p. 648.

4. Donald Guthrie, *New Testament Theology* (Downers Grove, Ill.: InterVarsity Press, 1981), p. 735.

5. Gene Getz, *Sharpening the Focus of the Church* (Chicago: Moody Press, 1974), p. 158.

6. Acts 21:18: "The next day Paul and the rest of us went to see James, and all the elders were present."

7. John R. W. Stott, *The Spirit, the Church, and the World* (Downer's Grove, Ill.: InterVarsity Press, 1990), p. 274.

8. Ibid., p. 236.

9. Scott, *The Lord's Day,* pp. 114, 115.

Chapter 4: Advantages of the Multi-Congregation Model

1. This figure is based on a report in *1992 Baptist Handbook* (Nashville: Baptist Sunday School Board).

2. Lyle E. Schaller, *Choices for Churches* (Nashville: Abingdon Press, 1990), p. 117.

3. I priced some land in our area at $100,000 an acre. There were seven acres for sale. It would seem reasonable to purchase all of this for a new church, assuming you were going to follow the traditional model. This would allow this church to plan facilities for 1,000 people. But it would require $700,000 to get started. This is prohibitive. We do not have that kind of up-front money to put into new churches. This great evangelistic tool is too expensive!

4. George Barna, *The Frog in the Kettle* (Ventura, Calif.: Regal Books, 1990), p. 135.

5. *The Quarterly Review* (July, August, September, 1989).

6. Leith Anderson, *Dying for Change* (Minneapolis: Bethany House, 1990), p. 159.

7. "Meet Southern Baptists" (1990 edition, 1989 statistics).

8. Ralph Neighbor, *Where Do We Go from Here?* (Houston: Touch Publications), p. 19.

9. Betty Lee Skinner, *Daws* (Grand Rapids: Zondervan, 1974), pp. 370, 371.
10. Peter Wagner, *Planting Churches,* p. 17.
11. Jackson Carroll and Robert Wilson, *Too Many Pastors? The Clergy Job Market* (New York: Pilgrim Press, 1980).
12. Schaller, *Choices for Churches,* p. 111.
13. Ted Engstrom, *What in the World Is God Doing? The New Face of Missions* (Waco, Tex.: Word), p. 198.
14. John Vaughan, *The Large Church* (Grand Rapids: Baker, 1985), p. 26.
15. Carl George, "Breaking the 800 Barrier" Seminar (1989).
16. Walter Mueller, *Direct Mail Ministry* (Nashville: Abingdon, 1989), p. 9.
17. I base this on a lecture by Rick Warren. I also understand from talking to marketing people that this is the norm throughout the industry. This explains why your mailbox is full every day. It works.
18. There is probably a mailing company in your area that can do this. You give them one piece of paper and circle on a map who you want to get it. Or you can give them zip codes or mail routes. You might even specify income level, number of children, and a host of other search criteria. They should be able to handle everything for you.
19. Schaller, *Choices for Churches,* p. 84.
20. From Robert Tucker, *Managing the Future,* quoted from a digest in *The Pastor's Update,* published by the Charles E. Fuller Institute of Evangelism and Church Growth, September 1991, p. 4.
21. Anderson, *Dying for Change,* p. 159.
22. Schaller, *Choices for Churches,* p. 87.
23. Ibid.
24. Barna, *The Frog in the Kettle,* jacket quote by Bill Hybels.
25. Ibid., p. 91.
26. Wagner, *Church Planting,* p. 28.
27. Ibid., p. 33.
28. Ibid., p. 11.
29. Ibid., p. 32.
30. Barna, *The Frog in the Kettle,* p. 139.
31. Schaller, *Choices for Churches,* p. 87.
32. Rowland Crowder, *Designing Church Buildings for Southern Baptist Churches* (Nashville: Convention Press, 1976), p. 41.
33. Bill Hybels, quoted by Timm Boyle, *Willow Creek,* September/October, 1990, p. 7.
34. Gustav Neibuhr, "Mighty Fortresses: Mega Churches Try to Be All Things to Busy People," *Wall Street Journal,* May 13, 1991.
35. Doug Murren, *The Baby Boomerang* (Ventura, Calif.: Regal, 1990), p. 145.
36. Jamie Buckingham, *Ministries Today,* September/October 1991, p. 4.
37. Charles Chaney and Ron Lewis, *Design for Church Growth* (Nashville: Broadman, 1977), p. 90.
38. This is the total estimated amount of capital assets the church in America currently possesses.

Chapter 5: Questions About the Multi-Congregation Church

1. George Wood et al., "Is There Life After a Building Program?" *Leadership,* Fall 1985, p. 127.
2. Elmer Towns, *How to Go to Two Services* (Lynchburg, Va.: Church Growth Institute, 1989), p. 9.
3. Peter Wagner, *Church Planting,* p. 27.
4. George Barna, *The Frog in the Kettle* (Ventura, Calif.: Regal Books, 1990), p. 143.
5. *Newsweek,* November 4, 1991, p. 20.
6. Barna, *The Frog in the Kettle,* p. 135.
7. Ibid., p. 121.
8. Ibid., p. 142.
9. Howard Snyder, *The Problem of WineSkins* (Downers Grove: InterVarsity Press, 1976), p. 21.
10. Ralph Neighbor, *Where Do We Go from Here?* (Houston: Touch Publications, 1990), p. 14.
11. Ibid., p. 19.
12. Gene Getz, *Sharpening the Focus of the Church* (Chicago: Moody Bible Institute, 1974), p. 160.
13. Roland Allen, *The Spontaneous Expansion of the Church* (Grand Rapids: Eerdmans, 1962), p. 12.
14. Ibid., p. 13.
15. Stott, *The Spirit, the Church, and the World* (Downers Grove: InterVarsity Press, 1990), p. 143.

Chapter 6: Principles on Change from the Book of Acts

1. Lyle Schaller, *The Change Agent* (Nashville: Abingdon, 1972), p. 11.
2. Ibid., p. 70.
3. Ibid., p. 71.
4. Ibid., p. 67, emphasis Schaller's.
5. Warren Bennis and Burt Nanus, *Leaders; Strategies for Taking Charge* (New York: Harper & Row, 1985), p. 27.
6. Ibid., p. 28.
7. Schaller, *The Change Agent,* p. 64.
8. Peter Wagner, *Church Planting for a Greater Harvest* (Ventura, Calif.: Regal, 1990), p. 45.
9. From the Institute in Basic Life Issues Seminar.

Chapter 7: Corollaries for Change Agents

1. I base this information on a video made available through Fuller Church Growth Institute. John Maxwell confirmed this information in a phone conversation.
2. Lyle Schaller, *The Change Agent* (Nashville: Abingdon, 1972), p. 65.

Chapter 8: Moving Toward a Multi-Congregation Model

1. Ernest Loosley, *When the Church Was Young.*

2. Gustav Neibuhr, "So It Isn't Rock of Ages, It Is Rock, and Many Love It," *Wall Street Journal,* December 19, 1991, p. A5.

3. James Montgomery Boice, *Nehemiah—Learning to Lead* (Old Tappan, N.J.: Revell, 1990), p. 55.

4. A common computer program that automatically calculates data based on predetermined formulas. The formulas are "hot," meaning that when you change a figure, you can learn immediately how the relevant factors will be affected.

5. George Barna, *User Friendly Churches* (Ventura, Calif.: Regal Books, 1991), p.22.

Chapter 9: Suggestions for Church Planters

1. Lyle Schaller, *44 Questions for Church Planters* (Nashville: Abingdon Press, 1991), p. 65ff.

2. Ibid., p. 72.

3. Taken from a conversation with John Vaughan.

Chapter 10: Our Story

1. Elmer Towns, from the packet, *"How to Go to Two Services."*

2. I said they were gracious enough to keep me, not that they did not slap my hand. I bear in my emotions the scars of those tragic days. As if that were not bad enough, I know I deserved it. For those I hurt, I can only stand in a posture of repentance and trust that their forgiveness is healing. If at all possible, avoid church fights. No one wins them. Turn the ship slowly.

3. If it has one at all. Not all churches make this distinction, but if they do make this distinction, the multi-congregation church will allow more than one. They may meet altogether from time to time, but it is not necessary for them to do so once a week.

Epilogue

1. Quoted from James Kouzes and Barry Posner, *The Leadership Challenge* (San Francisco: Jossey Boss Publishers, 1990), pp. 217, 248.

Appendix A: A Changing Population

1. Distributed by Ballantine/Del Rey/Fawcett Books.

2. Published by the Sunday School Board of the Southern Baptist Church, Nashville, Tennessee.